T0322491

MANAGING DIRECTOR Sarah Lavelle
COMMISSIONING EDITOR Stacey Cleworth
SENIOR DESIGNER Gemma Hayden
PHOTOGRAPHER Issy Croker
ILLUSTRATOR Evi-O.Studio | Emi Chiba
HEAD OF PRODUCTION Stephen Lang
PRODUCTION CONTROLLER Martina Georgieva

Published in 2024 by Quadrille,
an imprint of Hardie Grant Publishing

Quadrille
52–54 Southwark Street
London SE1 1UN
quadrille.com

Cataloguing in Publication Data: a catalogue record for this book is available from the British Library.

978 1 83783 083 1

Printed in China

OFF THE BEATEN TRACK

THE HIGHLANDS

Where to Eat, Sleep and Explore

MEG ABBOTT & ISSY CROKER

Hardie Grant
QUADRILLE

CONTENTS

INTRODUCTION

There's a word in Scottish Gaelic that is somewhat elusive, but seems to capture the essence of the Highlands better than any other. *Coorie's* meaning has shifted over the centuries, but generally refers to gathering energy, pleasure and wellbeing from the world around you – specifically, the wild landscapes and warm shelters of the Scottish Highlands. It's about finding comfort in nature, engaging with the present moment and finding joy in your surroundings – whether it's the crackling fire warming your bothy for the night, mountaintop views across a sparkling loch, or the cold, saline smack of a locally-caught oyster.

Coorie is a lovely word, even lovelier when you hear it spoken in a strong-as-single-malt Highland accent. But it is the feeling it describes that really sticks with you. One you can only start to understand when you're up in the highest point of Scotland, driving through mountain roads crawling with Crayola-yellow gorse, scaling the craggy edge of a 400 million-year-old mountain, watching the sunlight flash through the misty surface of a loch or sitting in an eighteenth century pub eating sweet scallops caught by the very fishing boat that bobs on the water beside you. Coorie isn't something you can take home with you – it is baked into life in the Highlands. And the fact that it is difficult to define seems fitting.

It is important to keep in mind that much of the vast emptiness of the Highlands is a result of what has become known as 'The Clearances', a dark period of Scottish history that gained momentum towards the end of the eighteenth century. During this social upheaval, many Highland communities – and their Gaelic culture – were uprooted and forced to leave their native land.

Isle of Skye

Today, many people are working hard to celebrate Gaelic culture and make it an integral part of the Highlands experience, for visitors and locals alike. Towards the end of the 1990s, the Scottish government began introducing Gaelic back to road signs across the region, so that now you can take a left turn towards Inbhir Nis (Inverness) or follow the A85 to Peairt (Perth). It's a small detail, but a continuous reminder of where you are, and the rich cultural history that is baked into the land. Yes, the Highlands is home to some of the most beautiful landscapes on Earth, some of the most friendly people you'll ever have the pleasure of meeting, prehistoric lands, ancient traditions and some of the world's most fascinating historical landmarks. But there is something more to the magic of the Highlands. And the only way to understand it is to feel it for yourself.

Issy and I are the first to admit that we are not nature people. The absolute darkness of a night sky in the wilderness makes us uneasy. The silence of a forest or hillside puts us on edge. The restful peace of living out in nature makes us restless. So setting off for a trip to the Highlands, home to the wildest and most remote region of the UK, we knew we would have to leave our overstimulated city selves behind and embrace life off the beaten track. No crowds, no traffic, no time pressure. No drama. But what we didn't realise about this part of the world is that it has its own kind of drama. The kind that nature writes for us. The Highlands and Islands is a vast land northwest of the Highland Boundary Fault, which crosses mainland Scotland in a straight line from Helensburgh to Stonehaven, and covers around 10,000 square miles in total, made up of towering mountains, peatlands, coastlines, farmlands and forests.

Piercing the edge of this region, you are greeted almost immediately with what is to come; the hills are soaring, the skies are wild, fast-moving and quick to bring bursts of sun or fits of storm clouds. The hills quiver with blankets of purple heather. When low, smoky clouds mist the mountains, the lochs are the colour of lead. And when the sun shines they glitter in shades

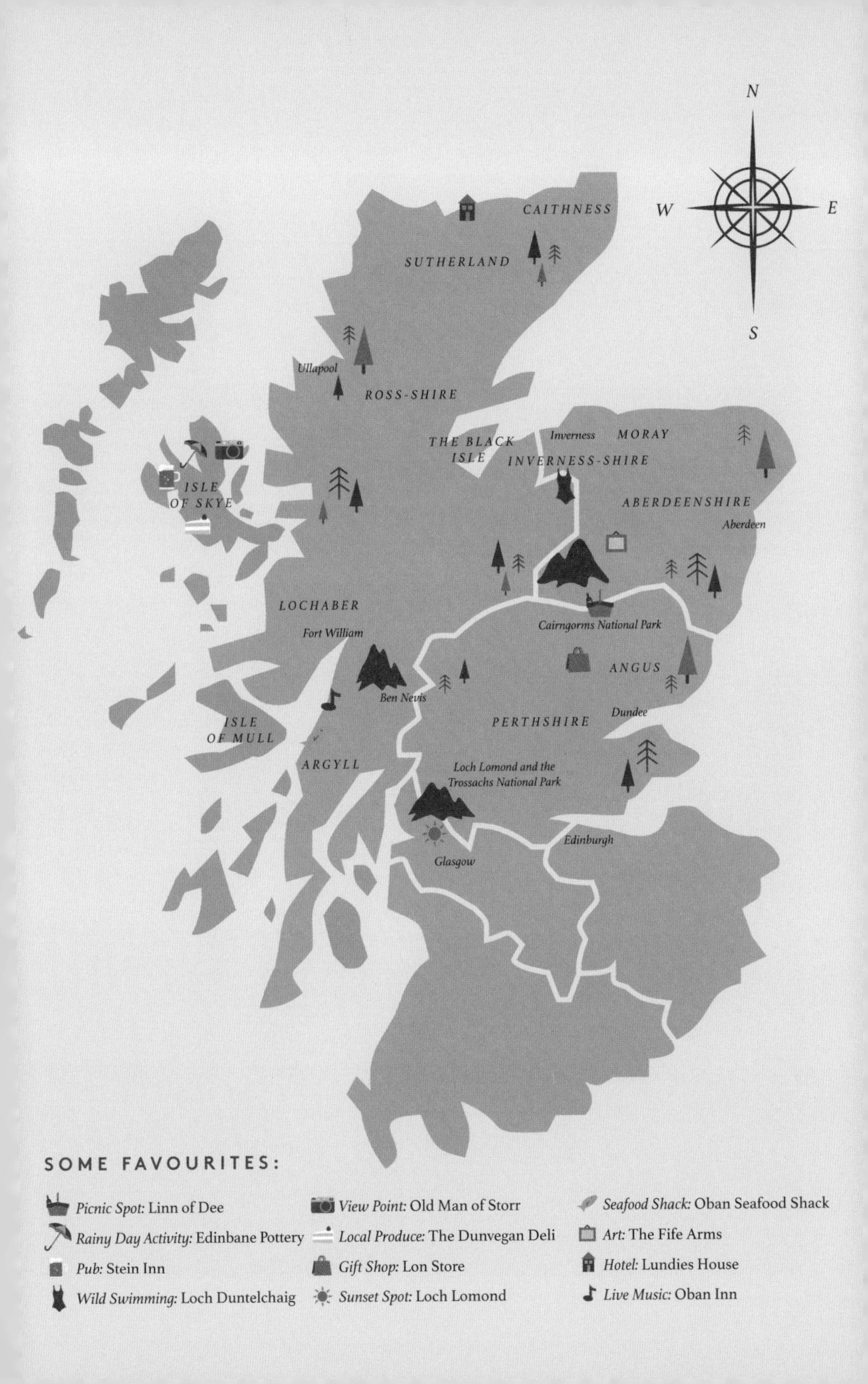
N
W
E
S
CAITHNESS
SUTHERLAND
Ullapool
ROSS-SHIRE
THE BLACK ISLE
Inverness
MORAY
INVERNESS-SHIRE
ISLE OF SKYE
ABERDEENSHIRE
Aberdeen
LOCHABER
Fort William
Cairngorms National Park
ANGUS
Ben Nevis
Dundee
PERTHSHIRE
ISLE OF MULL
ARGYLL
Loch Lomond and the Trossachs National Park
Edinburgh
Glasgow
SOME FAVOURITES:
Picnic Spot: Linn of Dee
Rainy Day Activity: Edinbane Pottery
Pub: Stein Inn
Wild Swimming: Loch Duntelchaig
View Point: Old Man of Storr
Local Produce: The Dunvegan Deli
Gift Shop: Lon Store
Sunset Spot: Loch Lomond
Seafood Shack: Oban Seafood Shack
Art: The Fife Arms
Hotel: Lundies House
Live Music: Oban Inn

of royal blue and lilac. The brighter the day, the more the loch mirrors the hills and sky above, doubling the drama. Deeper into the land you go, the roads turn from smooth tarmac to bouncy dirt track without warning. Herds of biscuit-coloured Highland cattle flock the roads, often prompting a standoff between driver (me) and pack leader (a giant, razer-horned bull with a ring in his nose). Swimming in the deep, cool waters here requires a deep breath and plenty of determination. Fresh oysters come salty, pearlescent and giant. Hilltop bothies offer no-frills overnight refuge for weary walkers. Centuries-old ruins remind us of the clans that once watched over the land. Whisky is strong and leaves your chest with a delicious heat. The landscape varies from snow-capped mountains and deep valleys, rolling farmland and rugged cliffs. The expansiveness of the land makes it the perfect choice for road trips, echoing the North American landscape that it was once connected to (600 million years or so ago). The Highlands may well embody 'slow living', but it is also a sensory experience to be here. There is something confronting about it. It asks you to pay attention, to tune in and look up. A few days into our trip, lying on a spongy moss at the end of a hill overlooking Loch Nell with the late evening sun shining through the trees, we came to an agreement; we could be nature people, after all.

GETTING AROUND

If you're able to drive, we highly recommend renting a car. The Highlands is the ultimate road trip destination, and driving means you can cover as much ground as possible, take in all the most dramatic landscapes and carve out your own unique journey. It's worth bearing in mind the vastness of this region. The Cairngorms National Park alone is twice the size of the Lake District National Park, so be sure to leave enough time to explore and plan well ahead if you're visiting with a strict timeframe.

If driving isn't your thing, there are plenty of train routes, including the famous Caledonian Sleeper and its Highlander Route between London Euston and Aberdeen, Inverness or Fort William, where you can hop off and continue exploring on foot – or find a bus to your next stop. Many consider The West Highland Line to be one the most scenic rail journeys in the world. The line runs from Glasgow north to Crianlarich, either running west past Loch Awe to Oban, or north through Rannoch Moor to Fort William and Mallaig. Buying a Spirit of Scotland Travelpass is a great option – it gives you four or eight days of unlimited travel on public transport for a fixed price. Find more information at *visitscotland.com/travel-planning*.

Stagecoach buses operate throughout the Highlands, covering Aberdeen city and shire, Buchan, Moray, Inverness, Badenoch and Strathspey, Caithness, Easter Ross, Sutherland, Orkney and Skye. You can plan your journey and check timetables on their website (*stagecoachbus.com*).

A 838
Durness 30
Kinlochbervie 48
Scourie 55

ABOUT US

We are Meg Abbott and Issy Croker, a writer and photographer duo who happen to have been best friends for 18 years. Issy has photographed food and travel for magazines such as *Vogue, National Geographic* and *The Sunday Times*. She's also shot cookbooks for the likes of Anna Jones, Gizzi Erskine and Jordan Bourke. I write for brands – everything from art and fashion to tech. And occasionally (when the world is being very kind to us), our love of travel and each other overlaps.

We are the first to admit our obsession with travel is out of control. Downright greedy, in fact. We're always on the hunt for the next fix – that one unforgettable meal, heady night, moment in nature or run-in with a wonderful stranger. We tend to choose the places furthest away, the more hours on a plane or sleepless nights of jet lag conducive to the biggest adventures. Over the years we've travelled side by side writing stories on markets in Morocco, coffee in Sweden, wine in Tuscany, pitmasters in Texas, street food in Tokyo, foraging in Finland and hiking trails in New Zealand. That last one ended with a mildly serious bicycle accident and a sprained ankle. But it was worth it for the view.

Driving through the ancient wilderness of Scotland's west coast, or hiking up the craggy edge of a mountain overlooking a sparkling loch, it seems so clear that such moments can be found far closer to home – right on our doorstep, in fact.

This is our second book together. We first celebrated The Lake District, and in this one we travelled the Highlands. We hope in this series we can share what we've learnt recently; that you don't always have to travel across the globe to find your next adventure.

Stac Pollaidh Walk

ABOUT THIS BOOK

This is by no means a complete guide to the Highlands; there's so much more for us to see. Rather, think of this as a snapshot of a long, meandering trip. We covered around 600 miles (965 km) by car, pulling over and jumping out whenever we saw a hill that begged to be climbed, a loch to lie beside or a village to explore.

We'd be lying if we said we had been meticulous with our itinerary. As tends to be our way when we travel together, we quickly found that having just a vague driving route, with no end goal in mind aside from our accommodation for the night, gave us the space to explore and change our plans according to what we discovered. We arrived with a handful of tips from friends who'd visited (and, in doing so, fallen in love with) the Highlands, but otherwise just let our instincts guide us.

We're celebrating this magical region by producing a curated guide with the best places to sleep, eat and explore. And we hope it arms you with a few must-see spots, and inspires you to explore the Highlands your way – whether you're someone who likes to plan ahead or leave things a little more open.

HOW TO USE THIS GUIDEBOOK

Travellers do not make their way through the world alphabetically, and neither does this book. In the upfront section of the guide, there are recommended routes as well as feature pages highlighting some of our favourite things to do.

The main chapters are ordered by area and you'll find our recommended places to sleep, eat and explore – these are by no means comprehensive, but a considered and thoughtful selection of our favourite places. Please note that the chapters do not all follow exactly the same pattern – the destination dictates what is and isn't included.

RESERVATIONS

While the Highlands is vast and often serenely empty, the more popular towns and villages do attract a lot of visitors, especially in the summer months. We recommend booking tables ahead of time, particularly for dinner. Seafood shacks and local cafés get busy, so be prepared to wait in line during the lunchtime rush. And make sure you check what time they shut so you don't miss out – once the last oyster is sold, they tend to shut up shop. We'd also recommend booking your accommodation at least a few weeks in advance (and a few months, in places like Skye), as many of the most magical only have a handful of rooms. Bothies are built for walkers, and you won't need to book ahead. But just be mindful that you likely won't be the only person in there, and fellow hikers can arrive later on in the evening. It's all part of the experience, and sharing is integral to bothy culture.

PRICES

We have featured some very special places in this guide, including some accommodation that is at a higher price point. Of course, if you're travelling on a stricter budget, bothies and camping grounds are a great choice. We have included a list of beautiful bothies, and for an extensive list of Highlands campsites, visit *scottishcamping.com*. Food- and drink-wise, we have tried to give a good range of choices, from fine dining options to classic pub grub and seafood shacks. The Highlands is one of those places you can spend a little or a lot, it just requires some planning.

HIGHLANDS ULTIMATE FIRST-TIMER'S PACKING LIST

'Four seasons in one day' is a phrase you'll hear a lot from Highlands locals. And it's true. You can set out for a walk on a drizzly, damp morning and be peeling off your layers in the sunshine by lunchtime. Rain can come storming in, seemingly out of nowhere. And you don't need to be in the region long to see the reason for that lovely local expression, 'blowing a hooley'. So it's best to pack for every eventuality, from dramatic storms to sweet sunshine, and everything in between. Trust us on this one.

- Small or large backpack
- Walking shoes
- Swimwear
- Insect repellent
- Sunglasses
- Thick socks
- Activewear
- Waterproof jacket
- Water bottle
- Lightweight blanket/picnic rug
- Suncream
- Thermos flask
- Portable phone charger
- Lightweight towel
- Corkscrew
- A camping stove
- Cutlery, plates and basic cooking equipment
- Blister plasters
- Binoculars
- Headphones
- Matches
- Map of the Highlands (in case you run out of phone signal!)

RECOMMENDATIONS

LOCAL MAKERS

There is a long history of making use of natural resources in the Highlands. Makers, artisans and artists are passionately upholding this tradition. This means you can visit ceramics workshops, tartan weavers and soap makers using the very same methods as their ancestors – and come home with pieces that vibrate with the essence of the place.

THE KILN CREATIVE

Based in Perthshire, Ellen Macfarlane's pottery can be purchased at local markets and is designed to last a lifetime. The Kiln Creative offers a range of pottery classes, where you can try your hand at throwing on the wheel, or building functional and sculptural ceramics by hand.

Mill of Muckly Farm Cottage, Dunkeld, Perth and Kinross PH8 0JF
@thekilncreativescotland

ARGYLL POTTERY

If you're passing through Oban, be sure to drop by and meet Hugh McTavish at Argyll Pottery. He has been working at this very kiln since 1988, crafting 'sturdy country pottery' that suits every kind of home.

Dallachullish Farm, Barcaldine, Oban PA37 1SQ

***Left to right**: Argyll Pottery, Edinbane Pottery, Skye Weavers*

LAURA THOMAS CO

Beautiful soaps, shampoos, candles and skin products made by hand in East Lothian using plant-based ingredients. Visit the shop on North Berwick high street, or look out for their brown glass bottles in stores across the Highlands.

laura-thomas.com | 67 High St, North Berwick EH39 4HG

SEA DRIFT POTTERY

Handmade ceramics inspired by the surrounding landscape. Beautiful bowls, vases and mugs are dashed with painterly blues and greens. Drop into their Argyll studio on the marina, and don't be surprised if you come out with more pottery than you can fit in your luggage. They also offer pottery workshops from March to October, including one-to-one sessions and larger groups classes.

seadriftpottery.com | Holy Loch Marina, Rankin's Brae, Argyll PA23 8FE

SKYE WEAVERS

Beautiful tweeds and textiles are woven inside a little weaving shed using a classic bicycle pedal-powered loom – which owner Andrea was kind (or brave) enough to let us pedal. With their unique tweeds, garments and homewares, she and husband Roger are working hard to preserve centuries-old textile traditions that are being lost in this part of the world.

skyeweavers.co.uk | 18 Fasach, Glendale, Isle of Skye IV55 8WP

EDINBANE POTTERY

Beloved for its vibrant, experimental glazes, Edinbane Pottery's distinctive style is created using both woodfired and a salt glaze kiln. They're open all year round for studio visits, where you can see the potters at work and leave with a few pieces of true Skye craftsmanship.

edinbane-pottery.co.uk | Edinbane, Portree IV51 9PW

LOCAL PRODUCERS

Highland producers have a genuine appreciation for the landscape around them. The region's relative isolation means they are well-versed in making use of local riches. Taking advantage of – and respecting – natural resources is a way of life here, so it's no surprise to find beautiful local produce at every turn. Patience, creativity and a dedication to sustainable practices are the inspiration behind all of these products, which we fell in love with during our travels. This list doesn't even scratch the surface, but it's a good place to start if you want a taste of the Highlands – and a slice of the place to take home with you.

HEBRIDEAN BAKER

Delicious bakes and bites from Scotland's best-selling cookbook author.

stagbakeries.co.uk/collections/hebridean-baker

ISLE MARTIN GIN

Fragrant, crowd-pleasing gin crafted with locally foraged botanicals from the uninhabited Isle Martin.

islemartin.org/isle-martin-2020-gin

DIGGERS CIDER

This beautiful bottled, modern craft cider is made using 100 per cent Scottish apples foraged from ancient orchards and local gardens in Perthshire. Minimal intervention is used, with nothing added but wild yeasts.

diggerscider.co.uk

SEVEN CROFTS GIN

This gin is responsible for both of us picking our G&T habits back up. It's fresh, crisp and fragrant, distilled using seven botanicals in a copper alembic still in the coastal town of Ullapool.

highlandliquorcompany.com/seven-crofts

BLACKTHORN SALT

Centuries of traditions are fused with modern sustainable practices to create these pristine table crystals, made nearby the harbour in Ayr.

blackthornsalt.co.uk

DANCING PUFFIN VODKA

Deliciously smooth vodka distilled in copper pots, celebrating the natural elements of Wester Ross and the surrounding landscape. You'll find it stocked in most good liquor shops.

badachrodistillery.com

THE DRINKS BAKERY

Andy Murray started baking at just ten years old. The Drinks Bakery creates delicious savoury biscuits to complement your favourite tipples, from Mature Cheddar, Chilli and Almond to Pecorino, Rosemary and Seaweed.

thedrinksbakery.com

FERAGAIA

Off the whisky? Feragaia is a hand-crafted alcohol-free spirit made using 14 land and sea botanicals, including lemon verbena, sugar kelp and pink peppercorn. It contains no sugar, is vegan and 100 per cent natural.

feragaia.com

BLACK PALM

Stock up on Black Palm's vegan skincare. Everything they make is natural and non-toxic, produced in small batches in Perth. Think aromatherapy candles, palm balm, natural deodorant and moisturiser.

blackpalm.co.uk

THE SCOTTISH BEE COMPANY

Celebrating the reciprocal relationship between land and food, The Scottish Bee Company produces beautiful pure honey, mixed with local plants like clover, rapeseed and Highland gorse, as well as salad dressings, hot honey and vinegar infusions.

scottishbeecompany.co.uk

MILK & HONEY

Small batch, handmade ice creams made using the highest quality ingredients. Try flavours like crème brûlée, cherry pie and vegan raspberry ripple by the scoop at Stirling locations including Blairmans Farm Shop & Coffee Bothy and Vera coffee shop.

milkandhoneyicecream.co.uk
@milkandhoneyicecreams

MUST-TRY SCOTTISH FOOD AND DRINK

Whether it's a fine dining dish, a plate of local fish or a towering stack of pub grub, food in the Highlands is more often than not made using local, seasonal ingredients. Most menus don't even call this out; it is just how they cook. And with this much lush, wild landscape and coastline, it's no surprise there's an abundance of fresh produce. Chefs across the region are getting creative with everything the land has to offer, but there are some Scottish staples that aren't to be messed with. Be sure to sample some of these classics while you're here.

CULLEN SKINK

The original recipe for this thick soup is said to have been written in the town of Cullen in Moray, on the far northeastern coast. In its most traditional form, it should be made using finnan haddie (thick pieces of hook-caught haddock), along with potatoes and onions.

CRANACHAN

Otherwise known as 'the king of Scottish desserts', cranachan was originally created to celebrate the raspberry harvest in June. It's a kind of trifle, made with oats, cream, whisky and raspberries. Instead of cream, purists will use crowdie – a soft Scottish cheese that has been made in the Highlands for centuries.

LANGOUSTINES

Sweet, pink and meaty, langoustines are one of the most luxurious – and abundant – shellfish in the Highlands. Most are from the North Sea and inshore waters, including the Moray Firth. You'll find them at most seafood shacks, on coastal pub menus and as the main event on fine dining menus.

SCALLOPS

Speaking of seafood, scallops are another delicacy you can't miss. Many restaurants are proud to get theirs directly from hand-divers. This is a sustainable way of offering the freshest possible scallops, which at their best should be deliciously plump and juicy.

TABLET

Think of this as Scottish fudge. This kind tends to be a little crumblier and grittier, made with butter, sugar and condensed milk. It's a centuries-old sweet treat, and you might even find it for sale from roadside honesty boxes along your journey. The perfect sugary pick-me-up.

WHISKY

If Scotland had a taste, it would be whisky. More precisely Scotch, which is locally-made malt or grain whisky. The options are endless, and whisky drinkers have strong opinions on what makes the perfect dram. The best way to approach the world of Scottish whisky is to visit a distillery. Join the Malt Whisky Trail in Moray Speyside for the ultimate whisky hop, or just ask at the bar of any pub you're in and sample a few local favourites.

***Left:** Inver Restaurant **Right:** The Dipping Lugger*

SCOTTISH PORRIDGE

A bowl of porridge is a simple but mighty thing. In Scotland, most people agree that salt should be added instead of sugar to give it depth and bring out the flavours of any toppings you add. And that it should be made with Scottish rolled oats, of course.

VENISON

If you see venison on a menu in the Highlands, the chances are it will be wild venison. It's one of the region's finest natural products, rich in flavour and beautifully lean. Our personal favourite venison dish was the Balmoral venison sausage roll at Tarmachan Cafe (see page 130).

SHORTBREAD

Apparently we have Mary Queen of Scots to thank for shortbread. It began as Medieval 'biscuit bread', made using leftover dough. These days it is synonymous with Scotland – the simple combination of flour, sugar, butter and salt creating a crumbly, moreish biscuit that goes perfectly with a strong cup of tea.

ARBROATH SMOKIES

Kind of like kippers, but made using milder, saltwater-dwelling haddock from the North Atlantic. Arbroath smokies are typically hot-smoked and their creamy, smoky flesh is a favourite addition to traditional cullen skink recipes (see page 26).

STOVIES

Good old meat and potatoes are a staple of Scottish cuisine. Stovies are a comforting muddle of meat (often using leftovers from Sunday's roast), onions, potatoes and stock. Some cooks like to add a little stout, too.

OAT CAKES

You'll find these classic crackers all over the Highlands. They are made using Scottish oats and the methods for making them haven't changed much in the last few hundred years. They're versatile enough to have with most dishes – from soups and stews to pâtés – or on their own slathered in jam.

HAGGIS, NEEPS AND TATTIES

The most classic (and therefore unmissable) Scottish comfort food. Traditionally served on Burns Night, this can be found on most pub menus in some form or another all year round. Haggis is made using the minced 'pluck' of a sheep (its liver, lungs and heart, to be exact), cooked with suet, oatmeal, spices and stock. It goes hand-in-hand with neeps and tatties – a creamy mix of mashed potatoes and turnips.

The Oyster Shed

SEAFOOD SHACKS

Eating fresh seafood, plucked straight from the coastal waters, is one of the joys of visiting the Highlands. Local pubs and restaurants are always sure to let you know the provenance of every fish dish, and eating local is par for the course. But the best way to sample the greatest selection of Scottish seafood is at a local seafood shack. Huts, shacks, shops and sheds; these places serve up the day's catches straight from fishing boat to plate. Come rain or shine, people flock to these spots to feast on local shellfish, succulent langoustines and sweet lobster. Usually served with a mountain of fat yellow chips and a giant wedge of lemon. Here are a few of our favourites, which you'll find in this book (read: places where we ordered enough seafood to feed a family of five).

Oban Seafood Shack (see page 48)

The Creel Seafood Bar (see page 65)

The Oyster Shed (see page 76)

Ullapool Seafood Shack (see page 90)

The Lobster Shop (see page 132)

The Seafood Bothy (see page 132)

***Clockwise from top left**: Guardswell Farm, Braemar Brewing Co, Fyne Ales Brewery Tap and Shop, Dewars Distillery*

BREWERIES AND DISTILLERIES

More and more breweries and distilleries are popping up across the Highlands. Drop by to see centuries-old whisky-making methods being upheld, and brewers foraging for local plants and flowers for exciting new craft beers. Pick up a few bottles for your next picnic, or to sample a couple of house favourites. Many of these places are family-owned, and there's always someone friendly to talk you through the latest creations. Here are the ones we came across on our travels.

BREWERIES

Fyne Ales Brewery Tap and Shop *(see page 56)*

Isle of Skye Brewing Co. *(see page 82)*

Black Isle Brewing Company *(see page 96)*

Cromarty Brewing Co. *(see page 99)*

Windswept Brewery *(see page 124)*

Cairngorm Brewery *(see page 125)*

Braemar Brewing Co. *(see page 139)*

DISTILLERIES

Springbank Distillery *(see page 56)*

Ben Nevis Distillery *(see page 60)*

Nc'Nean Distillery *(see page 61)*

Talisker Distillery *(see page 84)*

Glenfiddich Distillery *(see page 122)*

The Balvenie Distillery *(see page 125)*

Royal Lochnagar Distillery *(see page 136)*

Dewars Distillery *(see page 155)*

BOTHIES

There's something magical about the sight of a bothy. They stand alone on wild hilltops, waiting patiently for the next explorer passing through for the night. The word 'bothy' comes from the Gaelic *bothan*. Typically built with local stone and corrugated iron roofs, they originally served as shelters for farm labourers. They were rudimentary back in the day, and they still are. But what they all have in common is they can be found in some of the most memorable natural settings in Scotland.

Walkers heading to their next bothy shouldn't expect any frills. These isolated huts are free to stay in and left unlocked, so if you're staying you should expect other walkers to show up as well. Amenities are simple; there's usually a hard wooden sleeping platform, and no bathroom to speak of – bothies are typically close to a natural water source. Of the best known bothies, 81 are kept in check by the Mountain Bothies Association. This organisation was founded in 1956, based on the belief that walkers braving some of the Highlands' most rural locations should be rewarded with free shelter. They were also the ones to lay out The Bothy Code. In short, this code is all about respecting the bothy and everyone who joins you in it – and leaving it just as you'd like to find it.

Spending the night in a bothy, suspended in peaceful wilderness, is an experience everyone who visits the Highlands should have. Just be prepared to embrace the wilderness in its most remote, truest and tranquil form.

While the classic bothy experience is unmissable, there are more and more luxury options popping up around the Highlands for those who want to submerge themselves in nature – with all the comforts of a boutique hotel. Of course, the biggest difference is that classic bothies are free and therefore accessible to everyone, but if you did want to indulge in a high-end experience, we've included a few options. Invernolan (see opposite) is a great example of this.

See a map of bothies and plan your stay at mountainbothies.org.uk

Inverlonan bothy

BEACHES

There are a handful of beaches in the Highlands that feel like they don't belong there. They are the ones that appear like a mirage; white sand, pink cliffs, pristine blue waters disappearing into an endless horizon. There are others that feel very much like they should, those bookended by craggy rocks, splattered with pitch black seaweed and overlooked by sheep-filled hills – and possibly the odd seventeenth century church. Visiting a beach, maybe even two, should be part of your everyday plan while you're travelling the Scottish coast. In the summer, they cry out for lazy picnics and wild camping, and in the winter months you can wrap up warm, tackle the battering sea air on a beach walk and warm up after with a fireside whisky at a local pub. Here are the beaches we fell for on our trip – some famous and some a little harder to reach:

Kilbride Bay Beach (see page 56)

Westport Beach (see page 57)

Sanna Bay (see page 61)

Tràigh Gheal beach (see page 67)

Gruinard Bay (see page 96)

Ceannabeinne Beach (see page 110)

Oldshoremore Beach (see page 110)

Balnakeil Beach (see page 112)

Farr Beach (see page 112)

Strathy Beach (see page 112)

Findhorn Beach (see page 122)

Nairn Beach (see page 122)

Ceannabeinne Beach

WILD SWIMMING

Few things are more enticing on a hot day than the glistening waters of a loch. But before you dive in, make sure you have checked you're in a safe spot. Generally, you'll want to only swim in the summer months, when temperatures are milder and the days are long. The deep waters take a long time to warm up, and are actually only comfortable in late August or early September. Some lochs are incredibly deep and cold. While it's always tempting to jump in when there's no one else around, we recommend sticking to lochs that have more people in and around them. The depth of loch waters can change very suddenly, often in steep drops close to the shore. If you're not the strongest swimmer, make sure you stick to the edges and avoid jumping straight in before scoping out the depths. With all that in mind, it's one of the most pleasurable ways to spend an afternoon or sunny morning, so pack a swimsuit, light towel and bug spray (if you're visiting during the mid-May to September midge season) and submerge yourself in these clean, cool waters. Here are a handful of our favourite spots for swimming, floating on our backs or sunbathing on the water's edge.

LOCH DUNTELCHAIG

This magical Inverness-shire freshwater loch isn't peaty like your typical Highland loch. The water is crystal clear on sunny days, making it a popular spot for snorkelling – you'll be able to spot beautiful rock formations through the cool green water, some young vegetation and sunbeams streaming through the surface.

Nearest postcode: IV2 6AW

COIRE LOCH

The Cairngorms is brimming with wild swimming spots. This mountainous loch is Scotland's highest body of water. It's located 620 miles (997 km) above the Cairngorms, so prepare for a pretty tough hike to get there. It's worth it for the clear, gleaming freshwater though.

Begin your hike at: IV4 7LN

LOCH MORLICH

Another stunning wild swimming spot in the Cairngorms – this time without the hike. This is one of the busier lochs for swimmers, and you'll notice plenty of people setting up little campsites around the edges. It's still peaceful, though, with soft sandy shores and a dramatic backdrop of forest and mountains. It's relatively shallow and always busy with visitors, so it's a great option if you're new to wild swimming.

Nearest postcode: PH22 1QU

LOCH LOMOND

Lined by lush forests and towering mountains, Scotland's biggest freshwater loch is lined with sandy beaches and pebbly shores. Hire a mountain bike at Loch Lomond Leisure and hop on the West Loch Lomond cycle path, where you'll find some peaceful swimming spots along the way. Don't miss Milarrochy Bay, a picturesque stretch along the eastern shore.

Bike hire: lochlomond-scotland.com/activities/bike-hire/
Nearest postcode: FK17 8AA

LOCH VOIL

Located nearby Balquhidder Village, you'll reach this dreamy loch via a narrow, single-track road cutting through a dramatic glen, in a storied area known as Rob Roy country. Loch Voil is an isolated – and therefore usually very peaceful – freshwater loch where you can swim in utter peace with an extraordinary backdrop of mountains.

Park at Monachyle Mhor (where you can eat and drink after your swim): Balquhidder, Lochearnhead FK19 8PQ

RECOMMENDED ROUTES: SCENIC DRIVES

If driving is an option for you, be sure to factor in a road trip on your journey. We were amazed by the breadth and drama of this landscape, where pristine coastlines turn into volcanic glens, and thick forests open out into sprawling, russet-coloured mountains – sometimes so quickly you have to catch your breath. You'll want to get out and explore the beaches, pine-lined trails and hills on foot, but taking one of these cinematic drives is just as much of an adventure, and allows you to cover plenty of ground. We've covered the famous North Coast 500, plus a few more drives that will stick in your mind long after you leave.

For more scenic driving ideas, head to: visitscotland.com/inspiration/touring/scenic-driving-routes

NORTH COAST 500

(516 miles / 830 km)

Lots of visitors follow the North Coast 500, otherwise known as 'Scotland's Route 66'. This route loops around the north coast of Scotland, beginning and ending at Inverness Castle, leading you through what is arguably some of the most beautiful scenery on Earth. Travelling anticlockwise, you'll drive up the east coast from Inverness and Easter Ross, before exploring the wild north coast (including Cape Wrath and Durness) from Caithness. After that, you'll take in the stunning coast from Durness to Gairloch – dipping into some of Scotland's most spectacular beaches along the way.

FIFE COASTAL ROUTE

(77 miles / 124 km)

This is a much-loved walking path, but it's a dream to drive as well. It connects the River Forth and Tay Estuaries, tracing the golden coastline of Fife and passing by some of the Highlands' most scenic fishing villages – Elie, St Monans, Crail and Pittenweem, to name a few. Hop out at Tentsmuir Nature Reserve for a stroll through the woodlands, and head to the beach for fluffy sand dunes and sun-worshipping seals. Also, look out for seals sunbathing on the sands.

NORTH EAST 250

(250 miles / 402 km)

Depending on what you want to cover, this drive can take up to four days. It rivals the North Coast 500 in many ways, leading you over staggering mountain passes and through romantic seasides, with plenty of world-famous whisky distilleries and historic castles along the way. This 250 mile-long circular route begins in the heady wilderness of the Cairngorms, taking you through the rugged coastlines of the Moray Firth and on to Speyside whisky country. You can join the route at Glenshee, Aberdeen Airport or Ballindalloch.

ARGYLL COASTAL ROUTE

(129 miles / 208 km)

Beginning at Loch Lomond and ending at Ben Nevis, this stunning route has it all: ridiculously beautiful scenery, giant lochs, wildlife and island spotting. If you're lucky with the weather, you'll also be able to drink in the dramatic sunsets below the horizon on the west coast. You'll start on the 'bonnie banks' of Loch Lomond and The Trossachs National Park, before heading to world-famous Loch Fyne and Kilmartin Glen. After that, you can drop by Oban (also known as 'the gateway to the isles') for the region's best seafood, before exploring Glencoe and ending in Fort William, a bustling town in the shadow of Ben Nevis.

KINTYRE 66

(66 miles / 106 km)

Kintyre is a peninsula in the west of Scotland – one you may not have heard of, except in a Beatles song. It's brimming with history, and home to a mesmerising coastline. It's a great place to take to the water by boat (kayak or otherwise), sample the freshest seafood and marvel at haunting castles from some of the Highlands' most famous clans. It's a sweeping 66-mile (106-km) route, starting on the Atlantic road south. From here, you'll be able to see out to the islands of Islay and Jura. After that, you'll follow the edge of the Kilbrannan Sound overlooking Arran.

ISLE OF SKYE ROAD TRIP

(island circumference: 50 miles / 80 km by 25 miles / 40 km)

The best way to explore Skye is by car, tracing its undulating hills and craggy coastline. Not an 'official' driving route, but we suggest spending a couple of days here (you won't want to leave), letting your instincts lead the way. Be sure to factor in beautiful sights such as the Fairy Pools, Dunvegan Castle, Neist Point and Old Man of Storr, where you can get out and enjoy the hike that takes you to the epic pinnacle (see page 82).

RECOMMENDED ROUTES: PUBLIC TRANSPORT

The Highlands is more connected than ever, with great public transport routes to make your journey seamless – with a little forward planning, of course. Getting to the Highlands alone can be an epic journey, with magical routes from Glasgow, Edinburgh or London. There are plenty of buses to take you through some of the region's most staggering landscapes, and some train routes within the Highlands that are worth taking just for the scenery. Overall, it's surprisingly easy to journey around by bus and train. It gives you a lot of freedom to explore, and is a great option if you're travelling on a budget.

WEST HIGHLAND RAILWAY

There is so much to take in from the window, you'll likely get a sore neck after this train ride. Setting off from Glasgow, this famous line carries you north along the west coast, through Loch Lomond and the beautiful Trossachs National Park. It then splits at Crianlarich, taking you past Loch Awe to Oban or up to Rannoch Moor, passing through stunning wilderness on the way to Fort William and Mallaig.

scotrail.co.uk

THE JACOBITE STEAM TRAIN

This train line runs the final third of the West Highland Line. It's often described as the greatest railway journey in the world; an 84-mile (135-km) round trip starting near the mighty Ben Nevis, passing Loch Morar (the deepest freshwater loch in Britain) and the River Morar, finally arriving in Loch Nevis. It also crosses the 21-arched Glenfinnan viaduct, made famous in the Harry Potter films, overlooking the sparkling Loch Shiel. Be sure to book well in advance – tickets for this journey sell out fast.

westcoastrailways.co.uk/jacobite

STAGECOACH

Reliable and far-reaching, Stagecoach is a great option if you want to explore the Highlands by bus. These (mostly) punctual and (mostly) comfy coaches cover Aberdeen city, Buchan, Moray, Inverness, Badenoch and Strathspey, Caithness, Easter Ross, Sutherland, Orkney and Skye. Visit their website to take a look at the routes and book your tickets ahead of time (you can get a dayrider ticket in most zones).

stagecoachbus.com

CALEDONIAN SLEEPER

Dreamy in every sense of the word, the world-famous Caledonian Sleeper has become a rite of passage for Highland explorers. Travelling southbound from Scotland to London Euston, or northbound from London Euston to Scotland, you can snooze to the soothing sound of the passing countryside in your own private room. From London, the train splits into three at Edinburgh Waverley, journeying on to either Aberdeen, Inverness or Fort William. You can book your tickets up to 12 months ahead.

sleeper.scot

ARGYLL AND LOCHABER

ARGYLL AND LOCHABER

If you're beginning your journey in Glasgow, we recommend moving clockwise across the Highlands. Argyll and Bute boast the Highlands' most diverse landscape. Starting here gives you a dramatic taste of what is to come. It borders Loch Lomond and the Trossachs National Park to the east, and is near the charming Hebridean islands of Islay and Jura. Dense, fragrant forests lead to pristine sandy beaches and expanses of coastal wilderness. The region is well-known for its bountiful produce and whisky production, as well as the freshest fish plucked from the waters of the Atlantic or world-famous sea lochs. Boasting the most famous landmark of all, Lochaber is spread across a large portion of the western Highlands, with mighty Ben Nevis overlooking the town of Fort William. The area is also home to several islands, volcanic Glen Coe and miles of glittering coastline.

EAT AND DRINK

INVER RESTAURANT AND ROOMS

Standing in a former crofter's cottage and boat store on the shores of Loch Fyne, Inver is a celebrated restaurant breathing new life into traditional Scottish dishes with local wild and farmed ingredients that showcase the seasons. They bake their own sourdough, churn their own butter, and make their own ferments, preserves and ice cream in-house. They also roast their own coffee in an Argyll garage, and serve their own tonic syrup alongside local beers and natural wines. Tables are spread across stripped wooden floors, and huge windows make art of the views – including Old Castle Lachlan, a fifteenth century fortress across the water. They also have a handful of luxury shore-wide bothies, complete with king-size beds and bespoke furnishings. Stopping for lunch is a great idea, staying for the five-course tasting dinner is an even better one.

Strathlachlan, Strachur, Argyll & Bute PA27 8BU | inverrestaurant.co.uk @inverrestaurant

LOCH FYNE OYSTER

You'll find this restaurant just where the mountains meet the sea in Argyll. Inside this powder blue wooden building, locals and visitors fill up on 'west coast fruits of the sea'. Plump, creamy local oysters are the star of the show (of course), but leave space for lobster, buttery scallops and sweet langoustines too. Their seafood comes straight from Loch Fyne, and lots of it is finished in their in-house smokery. Best washed down with a bottle of Fyne Ales beer. You can also buy their luxurious smoked salmon – along with plenty of other delicious things – at their deli next door.

Cairndow PA26 8BL | lochfyne.com | @lochfyneoysters

CAMPBELL COFFEE

If you're stopping for a wander around the picturesque Inveraray on the banks of Loch Fyne, don't miss a cup of coffee at Campbell. All their coffee is produced on site and roasted by hand in small batches on a 10 kg Golden Roaster. They sell it in their signature bright orange bags if you feel like taking a batch home.

Main Street East, Inveraray PA32 8TP | campbellcoffee.com | @campbell_coffee

Inver Restaurant and Rooms

OBAN SEAFOOD SHACK

Don't miss the chance to feast on fresh-as-it-comes local seafood from this hut on Oban's Railway Pier. Otherwise known as 'The Green Shack' (not to be confused with others), it serves clattering bowls of hot mussels in white wine, lobster, oysters, shrimp and scallops. This place has been churning out affordable, delicious seafood since 1990. There's usually a queue, but it moves fast, and if the weather's on your side be sure to eat beside the fishing boats in the sunshine.

Calmac Pier, Oban PA34 4DB

EE-USK

This celebrated seafood restaurant sits on the shorefront in Oban Bay, with stunning views across the water to Kerrera and Lismore. All of their shellfish is locally sourced, including lobsters plucked from the rocky coast of Luing, Mull scallops and langoustines, mussels, and oysters from Loch Linnhe.

North Pier, Oban PA34 5QD | eeusk.com | @eeusk

OBAN INN

Stop by for a cold beer and some classic pub grub at this 18th-century inn overlooking Oban Bay. The town's most famous pub serves great beer, hand-selected whiskies, good coffee and big plates of fish and chips. They have regular live music sessions in the old style saloon lounge – and are proud to say they have no TVs. Which means chatting to locals over a few drams is always on the cards.

1 Stafford St, Oban PA34 5NJ | obaninn.co.uk | @theobaninn

HINBA COFFEE ROASTERS

We unapologetically doubled up on coffees here, they are that good. Hinba seasonally selects and roasts single origin specialty coffee 'in the pure Hebridean air' on the Isle of Seil. They pride themselves on staying true to local values, supporting the environment and the farms they work with. They care, and you can taste it.

62 George St, Oban PA34 5SD | hinba.co.uk | @hinba.coffee.roasters

Loch Fyne Oysters

Rain Bakery

RAIN BAKERY

Most visitors to this area pay a visit to the town of Fort William, where you can stock up on Scottish produce, walking supplies and fortifying food. A favourite is this bakery on the high street, run by former restaurant chef Steven Traill. Their flaky pain au chocolats are huge, and their cinnamon cruffins sell out every day. So get there in the morning and join the queue – it's worth it.

41 High Street, Fort William PH33 6DH | rainbakery.co.uk | @rain.bakery

THE WILDCAT

Also known as 'that vegan place', this friendly café serves homemade sandwiches, soups and salads bursting with good stuff, ethical coffee from Glasgow's Dear Green Coffee Roasters (using oat milk as standard), and lots of lovely organic groceries to take away. There are a lot of places in Fort William to eat haggis and sip beer, but if you're after a hit of health, this is the spot for you.

21 High St, Fort William PH33 6DH | @thewildcatfortwilliam

THE WHITEHOUSE RESTAURANT

The food at The Whitehouse, which overlooks Loch Aline, is deceptively simple. Their menu changes every day, reflecting the tiny changes in the seasons. Everything is sourced locally, or foraged by hand. Locals contribute too, with neighbour Lesley growing vegetables and Jamie down the road raising quail at home and giving The Whitehouse first dibs on the eggs. Bookings are a must, whether you're coming in for a two-course lunch or four-course dinner.

Lochaline, Oban PA80 5XT | thewhitehouserestaurant.co.uk
@thewhitehouserestaurant

SLEEP

MINKE CABIN

Named after the minke whales that you might be lucky enough to spot in the water, this luxury cabin sits in isolation on Davaar Island (accessed via a low tide causeway) in its own private glade overlooking the sea. It sleeps up to two guests, beautifully equipped with an ensuite bathroom, double bed, kitchen area and cosy wood panelling. The isolation of camping, with all the luxuries of a modern guesthouse. Bookings are for a mimimum of two nights.

Davaar Island, Campbeltown PA28 6RE | davaarisland.co.uk/minke-cabin @davaarislandcottages

INVERNOLAN

Chef Darren pointed out that the bothies look like a child's rendering of a house – the most organic, instinctual home there is. There are three bothies dotted along the water's edge, all fitted with Scandinavian-inspired touches such as wooden floors, limewash paint, wood burners and cosy beds with washed linen sheets. There's also a sauna for exclusive use by guests and you can access canoes and paddle boards. Follow the woodland path to the beach, where the waters of Loch Nell lap the shore.

To really get the full picture of this passion project, you must also have dinner there. A tasting menu of hyper-local Scottish produce is served in the original farmer's house, which most likely dates back to the sixteenth century. The building has been left in its original state, so stepping inside feels like winding back the clock a good 500 years or so. 'Do people usually cry when they see this?' I asked Darren. Inside, candles were flickering from cracks in the stone walls and two lanterns hung from the ceiling. The floor was covered in straw, and towards the back stood a table with a white cloth, chairs strung with fur blankets and a cup of sweet-smelling spring flowers. The evening light poured in through the slats in the ceiling, mixing with the smoke coming from burning charcoal outside. Anyone who knows either of us knows we are rarely lost for words, but we could do nothing but just stand and stare at this romantic, time-bending scene for a good five minutes. Then began one of the most unique, memorable, and frankly downright emotional dining experiences of our lives. Chef Darren Ross trained classically before working in the kitchen of Relae in Copenhagen.

Glenlonan, Oban PA34 4QE | inverlonan.com | @inverlonan

Invernolan

THE DRURY

This self-catered holiday home describes its style as 'country house cool'. The Drury is a Victorian mansion infused with all the modern comforts you need. It's a perfect option if you're basing yourself in Oban, which is the gateway to the west coast. Outdoor heated seats and fire pits mean you can sit under the stars for hours, and indoors you'll find cosy beds topped with Egyptian cotton sheets, a games room and even a cinema space. Sleeps up to 22 guests.

Dalriach Road, Oban PA34 5EQ | thedruryoban.com | @thedruryoban

EILEAN SHONA HOUSE

The classic facade of 'The House' on Eilean Shona, a car-free tidal island in Loch Moidart, is deceptive. Behind the heavy front door is a joyful maze of art-filled, kaleidoscopic rooms. Designed by celebrated architect Robert Lorimer and now owned by former art dealer Vanessa Branson, it fuses the luxury of a boutique hotel with the warm informality of a (very stylish) friend's house. There are nine bedrooms and six merrily-painted bathrooms, along with a canary yellow living room (complete with baby grand piano and plenty of Elton John sheet music), a classic snooker table and a well-stocked bar space finished in lucent orange. The house is self catered, and cooking in the duck egg blue kitchen is a pleasure in itself. The dining room is the most magical of them all, painted by the Glaswegian artist Fred Pollock in giant strokes of blue, orange and red. Elsewhere on the estate, there are eight self-catered cottages. Most of them are nestled on the southeast corner of the island, overlooking Loch Moidart and the ruins of the thirteenth-century Tioram Castle. All cottages are equipped with Egyptian cotton linen on the beds and fluffy towels in the bathrooms, and essentials such as kindling and a fire pit. On Tuesdays, everyone gathers at The Village Hall for a weekly pub night, where cocktails – and their very own Eilean Shona whisky – flow in front of a roaring fire from 6–8 pm. And if you want a peaceful space to get creative, an artists' studio is available to hire, perched on the banks of the loch. There's a small boat to pick you up from the mainland when you arrive, so pack everything you need for crabbing, wild swimming, painting, reading, hiking, picnicking and kayaking. This is island life, Highlands style.

Eilean Shona, Acharacle PH36 4LR | eileanshona.com | @eileanshona

Eilean Shona House

EXPLORE

WALK: WEST HIGHLAND WAY

Probably the most famous hiking route in the UK, the West Highland Way is a challenging walk that can take up to eight days. The 96-mile (164-km) route runs from the town of Milngavie, close to Glasgow, past Loch Lomond and over the Highland boundary line. After that, you'll walk through Glencoe and up to Fort William, the gateway to mighty Ben Nevis. The walk in its entirety is tough, so be sure to come fully prepared and feeling strong. If doing the entire walk feels a little intimidating (it definitely does to us), you can join the path on shorter routes along the way.

Information, kit lists and tips can be found at wildernessscotland.com/self-guided/walking/west-highland-way

SEE: KILBRIDE BAY BEACH

Lined by giant sand dunes, this crescent-shaped white sand beach lies on the southern coast of Tighnabruaich on the Kyles of Bute, with views across to the Isle of Arran. Brave the water, or nestle down on the sand and keep an eye out for seals, otters and porpoises.

Tighnabruaich PA21 2AH

DRINK: FYNE ALES BREWERY TAP AND SHOP

This family-owned farm brewery was founded in 2001. Since then, Fyne Ales have been brewing top-quality beer out of converted farm buildings on their 4500-acre estate, using water drawn straight from the surrounding hills in Argyll. Drop by to sample some of their classics like the Jarl Citra Session, or more unusual offerings like their 'spontaneous fermentation' beers, crafted with foraged ingredients like elderflower and liquorice mint.

Achadunan, Cairndow PA26 8BJ | fyneales.com | @fyneales

TOUR: SPRINGBANK DISTILLERY

Springbank's trademark single malt whiskies are produced in their distillery on the Kintyre Peninsula. There were once 30 distilleries in Campbeltown, but this is the last one left. Drop in for a tour, or pick up a bottle to take home. The royals are a fan, if you needed any more convincing...

Campbeltown PA28 6ET | springbank.scot | @springbank1828

SEE: WESTPORT BEACH

Admired by many as one of the west coast's most beautiful beaches, this 6 mile (9.5 km) stretch of pristine sand is made even more dramatic by the Machrihanish dunes that hug it – the biggest sand dunes in the region. The strong waves make it a popular beach for surfers, and it's always busy with dog walkers and picnic-ers in the warmer months.

Car park: PA28 6QD

HORSE RIDE: WILDER WAYS HORSE RIDING

Run by a former rural surveyor by trade and a specialist in renewable energy, Wilder Ways offer breathtaking riding adventures in the wilds of West Scotland. Choose from day rides and bespoke adventures for small groups to week-long holidays. Explore majestic hills, wild meadows, white sand beaches and mountains – including the odd swim on horseback.

Glen Kerran Farm, Southend, Campbeltown PA28 6PJ
wilderways.scot | @wilderways_adventures

WANDER: ARDUAINE GARDENS

In the spring, the gardens of the west coast burst into life. This peaceful garden brims with kaleidoscopic East Asian and South American flowers. The National Trust for Scotland oversees this colourful oasis, which is the perfect place to come for a stroll and to breathe in the coastal air.

Arduaine PA34 4XG | nts.org.uk/visit/places/arduaine-garden

SHOP: OBAN WHISKY AND FINE WINES

If you're planning a night in, grab a bottle of something special from this shop overlooking Oban Bay. They are experts in rare Scotch, particularly ones from the West Coast. You'll find limited edition and single malt whisky from all the iconic distilleries around Scotland, along with lots of interesting wines.

19 Stafford St, Oban PA34 5NJ

The Modern Croft

SHOP: THE MODERN CROFT

This hidden gem beside Oban's North Pier showcases a curated selection of handcrafted ceramics, textiles, skincare and household items. The Modern Croft celebrates Scottish heritage with a contemporary twist. Supporting local artisans and sustainable practices, it provides a glimpse into Oban's vibrant creative culture.

North Pier, Oban PA34 5QD | themoderncroft.com | @themoderncroft

WANDER: GLENCOE

Dedicate a day to exploring this stunning village. It's situated in Glencoe valley, an area that's famous for its dramatic waterfalls and hiking trails. It's also home to Glencoe Mountain Resort, a ski resort operating on Meall a' Bhuiridh mountain, with sweeping views over Buachaille Etive Mor from the slopes. If you're looking to ski, January to mid March are the best months. It's a great place to visit all year round, though. See the Three Sisters three mountain peaks on the Lost Valley Hike (or appreciate them from your car), visit the sparkling waters of Glencoe Lochan, visit a classic pub or feast on fresh catches from Lochleven Seafood Café (closed in the winter).

WALK: BEN NEVIS

You'll already be familiar with this iconic mountain. What we didn't realise was just how massive (and magnificent) it is. This is the highest mountain in the UK, looming over the Grampian Mountains in Lochaberonce. It was once a giant active volcano, exploding and collapsing in on itself millions of years ago. The nearest town is Fort William, where you'll notice lots of walkers gearing up for their ascent or celebrating their climbs in the local pubs. Climbing to the summit and back takes around seven hours, so it's not for everyone. A breezier option is the River Nevis Walk, which leaves from the same car park and follows the river bank, allowing you to explore Lower Glen Nevis in around an hour if you're not up for the full climb. We won't lie, we went with this option.

Car park: Visitor Centre, Glen Nevis, Fort William PH33 6ST

SHOP: THE HIGHLAND SOAP COMPANY

You'll find Highlands Soap Company stores in a few locations across the region, but if you want to see what makes this family-run company tick, head to their workshop. Tucked between River Lochy and the thirteenth-century Old Inverlochy Castle, it's set in six acres of grounds and gardens with views over Ben Nevis. All their soaps are made using centuries-old techniques, using Highlands produce. Drop in for a factory tour, or try your hand at making your own soap.

Inverlochy Mains, Old Inverlochy Castle, North Road, Fort William PH33 6TQ
highlandsoaps.com | @highlandsoapco

TOUR: BEN NEVIS DISTILLERY

You'll find this imposing distillery at the foot of Ben Nevis, the highest mountain in the UK. Founded by John 'Long John' MacDonald, this is one of Scotland's oldest licensed distilleries. They have been crafting malt whisky from the highest water source in Scotland since 1825, and have stood strong as one the country's favourite whisky producers.

Lochy Bridge, Fort William PH33 6TJ | bennevisdistillery.com
@bennevisdist

SEE: GLENFINNAN VIADUCT

Glenfinnan Viaduct was known first as a feat of Victorian engineering and the longest concrete railway bridge in Scotland, but more recently has been made famous as the bridge carrying the Hogwarts Express in the Harry Potter films. The best view is from the ground, where you can see the Jacobite steam train running along the hillside and crossing the Viaduct in a puff of smoke. You can view all this from the roadside, or from the most popular viewing point on the hillside near the northwestern tip. Reach it by following the path from the road and under the arches or by taking the trail from Glenfinnan station.

Glenfinnan PH37 4LT

TOUR: NC'NEAN DISTILLERY

There is no shortage of whisky distilleries in this part of the world; but Nc'nean is doing things a little differently. This young, independent, organic whisky distillery is crafting experimental spirits using Scottish barley in a distillery powered by renewable energy. Their creations are bottled in 100 per cent recycled clear glass bottles. Be sure to sample their inventive classics such as the Botanical Spirit or Aged Botanical.

Drimnin, By Lochaline, Morvern PA80 5XZ | ncnean.com | @ncnean

SEE: SANNA BAY

Stumbling upon pristine white sand beaches is one of the joys of exploring the Highlands. Sanna Bay is one of the most beautiful, situated on the Ardnamurchan Peninsula in the most westerly point in mainland Britain. But on sunny days, it looks like a slice of the Caribbean. There are views of the Isles of Rum, Muck, Eigg and Canna from the shell-flecked sand, and if you stay long enough, you will probably catch a glimpse of dolphins and whales in the turquoise water.

Car park: Acharacle PH36 4LW

ISLE OF MULL

ISLE OF MULL

Snoozing on the west coast of Scotland, Mull is the second largest island of the mystical Inner Hebrides. Compared to some of the other islands, Mull has a gentler, less dramatic landscape. Its west coast is peppered with rugged cliffs, and we're told this is the best place to view majestic golden eagles. The lack of air pollution makes it home to one of the darkest skies in Europe, so stargazing is a pastime for visitors to Mull. Many creatives have made their home here, drawn by the tranquillity and simplicity of the island. Tobermory is the friendly main town, but you'll get a deeper sense of the island if you stay further afield. Pack some good walking shoes and explore the patchwork of forests, moors, hills, coastlines and glens on foot.

EAT AND DRINK

ISLE OF MULL CHEESE AND THE GLASS BARN

Sgriob-ruadh Farm is a dairy farm with a history dating back to the 1980s; they produce award-winning unpasteurized cheeses, including the much-loved Farmhouse Cheddar and Hebridean Blue. The farm's 130 dairy cows provide the milk, and are fed on spent grains from Tobermory Distillery. Sample their experimental cheeses in their Glass Barn café and farm shop, along with other signature products like their pork – made from pigs fed with the whey from cheese making.

Sgriob-ruadh Farm, Tobermory, Isle of Mull PA75 6QD
sgriobruadh.co.uk | @the.glass.barn.mull.cheese

THE CREEL SEAFOOD BAR

Feast on seafood caught locally in the surrounding waters of Mull and Iona at this blue seafood shack. Think huge bowls of mussels, scallops, creamy seafood chowder and squid, eaten on benches looking across the water to Iona.

8 A849, Isle of Mull PA66 6BL

CROFT 3

Croft 3 is a working croft and seasonal restaurant. With a focus on simplicity and sustainability, their small, seasonal menu celebrates local produce from the island, and their goal is to become completely self-sufficient. Feast on reworked classics such as haggis, neeps and tatties with whisky sauce, crab orzo with fennel and saffron, and gin and tonic sorbet with a ginger crumble. On Sundays they serve roasts – which should always be finished with their perfect sticky toffee pudding.

Isle of Mull PA73 6LX | Croft3mull.co.uk | @croft3mull

SLEEP

LINNDHU HOUSE

Linndhu House is a renovated Edwardian country house set in 27 acres of private grounds. This charming B&B still has lots of original features of the period, but has been lovingly restored with five cosy en-suite rooms available. Their lovely breakfasts are the perfect way to kick off a day exploring the Isle of Mull. Minimum stay of two nights.

Linndhu House, Tobermory, Isle of Mull PA75 6QB
linndhuhouse.com | @linndhuhouse

EXPLORE

WALK: AROS WATERFALLS

Kicking off from Tobermory, this half-hour hike from the car park takes you through a woodland brimming with lush ferns and waterfalls. There are also panoramic views of Mull's port town, Tobermory, across the bay to Calve Island and to the cliffs of Morvern.

Ledaig car park: Tobermory, Isle of Mull PA75 6NR

SEE: TRÀIGH GHEAL BEACH

Gaelic for 'white beach', this is one of Mull's most secluded spots. It's located on the south coast of the island, and you can walk to it from Fionnphort. Park at Knockvologan Farm and take the road to Fidden. If you go through the gate at the side of the farm buildings, you'll find maps in an honesty box attached to the gate. From here, it's around a two hour hike through the boggy, wild Tireragan Nature Reserve to get to the beach.

Knockvologan Farm car park: Knockvologan, Isle of Mull PA66 6BN

WANDER: IONA ISLAND

Iona is a 'tiny wee island' off the west coast of Mull, and makes for the perfect afternoon trip. Hop on the 10-minute ferry from Fionnphort, and spend a few hours exploring this serene spot. It's only 3 miles (4.8 km) long and 1 mile (1.6 km) wide, so it's a beautiful place to wander (aimlessly, in our case). It's known for Iona Abbey and Nunnery, and the village can get pretty busy in the summer months. Break away from the crowd by slipping off to the silvery beaches to the west of the island.

PA76 6SJ

ISLE OF
SKYE

ISLE OF SKYE

Everyone who visits the Isle of Skye seems to come away with the same feeling; there's something very special in the air here. Maybe it's the rolling green hills, sleepy settlements and sparkling coastline. Or the way its peace leaves you with all the time and space to unwind, unplug and reset. Ancient traditions or craft and cooking are nurtured here, from tartan weavers using machinery passed down the generations to whisky being made in the same way it has been for hundreds of years. This serene island has a tight knit community, and its proud residents are always keen to share their local secrets – and their love for the place – with you. It's hard to leave the Isle of Skye. It has that rare effect of making you feel completely at home and also like you've stepped into another world entirely. One thing is for sure, we'll be back.

EAT AND DRINK

THE NOOST

Handily positioned beside the Raasay ferry terminal at Sconser, this lochside café serves elevated, seasonal café food. Stop by for great coffee, artisan ice cream (or, even better, affogato), vanilla and coconut iced lattes, and sandwiches with baked ham, wild rocket and mature Cheddar, or fresh poached salmon and lemon mayo on a golden hoagie.

Sconser, Isle of Skye IV48 8TD | @thenoostskye

BIRCH

Minimalist, serene and finished with crafted wooden furniture, Birch is inspired by the café culture of Melbourne. Have a stroll around Portree and end with a perfect flat white in their sunny window. They opened their roastery in 2021, with a commitment to tracing their coffee back to the source and using produce from the Scottish Highlands and islands.

Bayfield Rd, Portree IV51 9EL | birch-skye.co | @birch_skye

SCORRYBREAC

'Scorrybreac' means 'speckled rock', inspired by the stoney cliffs just along the bay from this Portree restaurant. They get their fish from local fishermen, and source their wild venison, foraged plants and shoreline sea vegetables from the surrounding land. The menu changes constantly, but expect delicate, artful dishes bursting with Scottish flavours. Best finished with a dram of Single Malt, of course.

7 Bosville Terrace, Portree IV51 9DG | scorrybreac.com
@scorrybreacrestaurant

EDINBANE INN

Make this traditional inn your last stop after a day exploring Skye. Settle in next to the fire and sample some traditional Scottish dishes such as Hebridean mussels with garlic, white wine, cream and crusty bread, wild Skye venison burgers or slow cooked Scottish beef. Catch live music on Wednesdays, Fridays and Sundays if you can.

Edinbane, Isle Of Skye IV51 9PW | edinbaneinn.co.uk | @edinbane_inn

Birch

Stein Inn

STEIN INN

We ate a lunch of buttery langoustines and plump monkfish at Stein Inn, looking out through the window at Loch Bay, where the very fishing boat that caught the seafood for us bobbed in the sun. Dating back to around 1790, this is the oldest inn on the Isle of Skye. The interior is filled with colourful, homely touches and eye-catching artworks, and on warmer days you can eat outside on the banks with views towards the Outer Hebrides. 'Everything is simply done and super fresh,' owner Charlie tells us. 'When the fish is this fresh, you just want to taste the sea.'

Macleods Terrace, Stein IV55 8GA | thesteininn.co.uk | @stein_inn

THE DUNVEGAN DELI

Stock up on eco cleaning supplies, organic soaps and Dear Green coffee beans from their Glaswegian roastery at this conscientious deli/refillery. Next door is their restaurant, where locally sourced Scottish ingredients are cooked over fire, inspired by Argentinian cooking techniques.

Main Street, Dunvegan, Isle of Skye IV55 8WA | thedunvegan.com
@dunvegandeli

THE THREE CHIMNEYS

Whether you're settling in for a tasting menu and whisky pairing, or going à la carte, prepare for a very memorable meal. Perched on the shores of Loch Dunvegan, The Three Chimneys is a restaurant honouring the landscapes and seascapes of Skye. Inspired by ancient Nordic and modern Scottish techniques, head chef Scott Davies and his team use local ingredients such as langoustines and crab from Loch Dunvegan, Loch Creran oysters, Armdale Estate deer and locally foraged mushrooms.

Colbost, Dunvegan, Isle of Skye IV55 8ZT | threechimneys.co.uk
@thethreechimneysskye

CAORA DHUBH COFFEE

Another excellent coffee stop on the Isle of Skye. Caora Dhubh (Gaelic for 'Black Sheep') serves coffee from independent roasters across the Highlands. Operating out of a minimalist wooden cabin on the banks of Loch Harport, they use the finest equipment to make the best cup of coffee possible.

Carbost, Isle of Skye IV47 8SR | caoradhubh.com | @caoracoffee

CHIDAKASHA TEAHOUSE

Restore yourself after a day's walking (or a day lying on the shores of the loch, in our case) at this tranquil vegetarian restaurant on a quiet hillside in Glendale, northwest Skye. A set menu is cooked every evening in the small kitchen, with an accompanying tea tasting. The blend of candlelight, cooking smells and quiet chatter is blissfully calming. So much so that it's difficult to leave. Definitely book a table – they have two dinner slots every evening, and they fill up fast.

Holmisdale, Glendale, Isle of Skye IV55 8WS | chidakashaskye.co.uk @chidakashaskye

THE LEAN TO

This roadside café is located in an old stone family croft and artisanal coffee is served from a converted shipping container. Their coffee is a variety of locally roasted beans and they source the best ingredients for everything from their breakfast bowls to their honey-soaked sticky chai – plus they stock flaky Mallaig bakery pastries.

8, Ashaig, Isle of Skye IV42 8PZ | @leantocoffee

THE OYSTER SHED

Don't leave Skye without lunch at this popular seafood spot. Queues form early for lunches of freshly caught lobster, hot smoked salmon, scallops and freshly shucked oysters. You can also pick up local produce such as smoked Scottish game, cheeses and chutneys from their store. They don't charge corkage, so you can also bring your own bottle if the mood strikes.

Carbost Beag, Carbost, Isle Of Skye IV47 8SE | theoystershed.com

The Lean To

SLEEP

KIP HIDEAWAYS: WEST COAST CABIN

This contemporary cabin can be found down a bumpy track, standing serenely at the edge of a heathery cliff overlooking Loch Pooltiel. It sleeps eight people, with a tranquil and airy living space complete with a big dining table, cosy sofas, fully-equipped kitchen and a wood burner. The floor to ceiling windows make the dramatic views the centrepoint. Sheep graze in the grass, the cliffs plunge into the loch and the mountains of the Outer Hebrides stand misty and blue across the water. Skye has a lot to offer, but it can be somewhat of a challenge to leave this place.
You can walk from the porch to the edge of the cliffs with the pristine water lapping the shore, which turned out to be the ideal place to bathe in the evening sunlight. If it sounds a little too idyllic, that's because it is.

By Glendale, Isle of Skye (exact location shared on booking)
Kiphideaways.com | @kiphideaways

HAME HOTEL

Another 'Scandi-Scot' creation, this single-storey hideaway is located on Skye's northwest coast. It faces a field leading down to Loch Vatten, a few miles from Dunvegan Castle. A couple from Hackney renovated this former hospice, decking it out with wooden cladding, wide windows and a lounge bar. There are eight rooms in total, all finished in soothing muted tones and bespoke finishes. A small but thoughtful menu is served at Hame Kitchen, with a focus on beautiful local produce.

Roag, Orbost, by Dunvegan, Isle of Skye IV55 8GZ | hameonskye.com

HARLOSH BLACK H

The black cladding of this minimalist house is striking against the rugged beauty of the open croft that surrounds it. Inside, it's clean and spare, with warm oak touches. There are views of the sea and the curious Macleod's Tables flat-topped hills. Sleeping two, this secluded hideaway is the perfect place to unwind, unplug and take in the beauty of Skye – with all the luxuries you could need.

4–5 Ardmore, Dunvegan, Isle of Skye IV55 8ZJ | @harlosh.co

Kip Hideaways: West Coast Cabin

CORUISK HOTEL

Coruisk Hotel is a restaurant with rooms on the Isle of Skye, specialising in seasonal dishes, hand-picked wines and local whiskies. You'll reach the hotel on a 13-mile (21-km) single track road, down the glen around the loch to Elgol. The main hotel is a cosy mix of lime-washed walls, antique furniture and vintage fabrics, while the rooms include slipper baths (in The Steading), huge beds and locally-crafted mohair throws. Take in views of the magnificent Cuillin mountain range from nearby Elgol harbour, where you'll be able to hop on a boat trip to Loch Coruisk and the Small Isles of Rum and Canna in the Inner Hebrides.

26 Elgol, Isle of Skye IV49 9BL | Coruiskhouse.com
@coruiskhouse

KINLOCH LODGE

Kinloch Lodge Hotel and Restaurant is a former hunting lodge, and has been a family-run hotel for five decades. This is a classic taste of the Highlands, standing in all its seventeenth-century glory on the shores of Loch Na Dal. The colourful, warm interior is peppered with antiques and oil paintings, and you can nestle down by the fire (preferably with a whisky) in their cosy living room. The restaurant is at the heart of Kinloch. Chef Jordan Webb does all the gardening, growing delights such as thyme, gooseberries, raspberries, lovage, chard and French breakfast radishes on the grounds. 'We pick them and they're on the plate within 10 minutes,' he tells us. Guests can also join their ghillie ('custodians of the countryside') Mitchell Partridge for a forage on the loch's shore, or a fishing trip on the water.

A851, Sleat, Isle of Skye IV43 8QY | Kinloch-lodge.co.uk
@kinloch_lodge

Portree

EXPLORE

WALK: OLD MAN OF STORR

If you only have time for one walk, this is a stunning option. The iconic Old Man is one of the most photographed landscapes in the world, made up of a huge formation of standing rocks in an area known as Trotternish. Follow the clearly marked 2⅓-mile (3.8-km) Storr walk, where you'll take the same path there and back. It takes just over an hour, depending on how much time you spend marvelling at the views from the top.

Car park: Portree IV51 9HX

SHOP: ISLE OF SKYE BREWING CO.

Dreamt up by some friends in a local pub back in 1992, Isle of Skye Brewing Co. have picked up many awards for their balanced, creative beers, all made in their brewery set in the dramatic landscape of Skye. They nurture ancient traditions, innovating classics with seasonal ingredients hand-picked on the island. Pay a visit to their site in Uig to hear more about the process, and pick up a bottle or two.

The Pier, Uig, Isle of Skye IV51 9XP | @isleofskyebrewery

WALK: GLEN SLIGACHAN

One of the most beautiful hikes in Skye, and quite possibly in the entire Highlands. It's a tough one – around 7½-miles (12.5-km) one way. But if you have time, and are feeling strong, it's worth it. This long, peaceful glen is essentially a deep pathway between Skye's two great ranges, dividing the Red and Black Cuillin mountains and running from sea to sea. You'll be able to take in the dramatic, craggy beauty of the mountains throughout the walk, as well as pass a collection of little lochs (perfect for a dip, if you're in the mood).

Car park: Sligachan Old Bridge, Sligachan, Isle of Skye IV47 8SW

SEE: THE CORAL BEACHES

While Skye has around 311 miles (500 km) of coastline to its name, there are only a handful of sandy beaches. This one, near the village of Claigan, has turquoise waters and bright white sand formed by crushed, coral-like seaweed. You can only reach these two beaches on foot, so leave your car at Claigan and walk 1½ miles (2.4 km) through a beautiful protected nature reserve.

Claigan, Dunvegan, Isle of Skye IV55 8WF

Glen Sligachan

SEE: SKYESKYNS

Leather making is one of the oldest crafts in Scottish history, and you can get a taste of the craft in its traditional form at Skyeskyns' tannery on the Waternish Peninsula. Join the tour to see classic implements used by the Tanner: the beam, paddles, racks and buffing wheel, which all go into creating Highland hand-combed fleece exclusive to Skyeskyns. There's also a shop where you can buy throws, rugs and even hats.

17 Lochbay, Waternish, Isle of Skye IV55 8GD | skyeskyns.co.uk | @skyeskynsltd

TOUR: TALISKER DISTILLERY

This is the oldest working distillery on the islands, perched on the shores of Loch Harport overlooking the rocky Cuillin mountain range. Join one of their hour-long immersive tours (complete with tastings, of course) to understand more of the distillery's history, flavour and traditional production processes.

Carbost, Isle of Skye IV47 8SR

WALK: FAIRY POOLS

These mystical rock pools in Glenbrittle are known as the Fairy Pools. This translucent mountain spring water is delivered by a series of waterfalls from the Cuillin Mountains. From the Fairy Pools car park, it's a 1½-miles (2.4-km) walk to the water. Some people are brave enough to take a dip, but be sure to bring a wetsuit and take care on the rocks if you do – the water is beautiful but freezing.

Car park: Glenbrittle, Isle of Skye IV47 8TA

BOAT: BELLA JANE BOAT TOURS

Join the wonderful team behind this award-winning boat touring company, which offers sightseeing and wildlife tours to Loch Coruisk and the Small Isles – typically from the beginning of April to the end of October. Departing from Elgol, you'll visit the Cuillin mountains, and see the seals bathing on the rocks. If you're lucky, you might even catch a glimpse of minke whales, dolphins, porpoises or sea eagles. Choose from a three-hour standard return trip, which includes time ashore at Loch Coruisk, or a non-landing trip of around an hour if you want to stay aboard. You'll get refreshments such as tea and coffee on your return, and if your hat happens to blow into the sea, the lovely skipper will be happy to retrieve it from the waves for you. Thanks again, Nick...

Elgol Pier, Isle of Skye IV49 9BJ | bellajane.co.uk | @bellajaneboattrips

Bella Jane Boat Tours

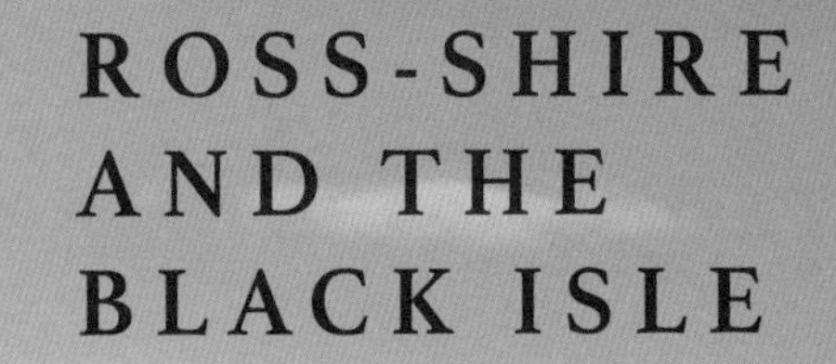

ROSS-SHIRE AND THE BLACK ISLE

ROSS-SHIRE AND THE BLACK ISLE

If you're heading toward Skye, make sure you stop off in Ross and Cromarty. It's one of the northernmost points of the Highlands, well known for its wild natural beauty, and spans the width of Scotland from the North Sea on the east to the Atlantic Ocean on the west. Its deep lochs are a haven for wild salmon fishers, and it's home to the lively town of Cromarty and colourful, coastal Ullapool. On the east coast The Black Isle is, despite its name, a peninsula surrounded by water on three sides. This region is greener than some of its neighbours, is rich in farmland and a great place to spot wildlife such as deer, dolphin and otter. You'll find history-drenched castles overlooking misty waters and towering cairns here, along with dense woodland full of bonsai pines and dragonflies.

CROMARTY POST OFFICE
POST OFFICE
Welcome

EAT AND DRINK

THE CEILIDH PLACE

If you're lucky enough to be in Ullapool on a sunny day, stop by this buzzy pub for a drink in the sun. As well as being an excellent boozer, this is also a restaurant, bookshop and live music venue. Their bar is stocked with all the good stuff, including Seven Crofts Gin (from the team behind The Dipping Lugger, see page 94), local beers and the finest whiskies.

14 West Argyle Street, Ullapool IV26 2TY | theceilidhplace.com @theceilidhplace.com

CULT CAFE

Cult Cafe brings a slice of sunny New Zealand café culture to (slightly less sunny) Ullapool bay. This is a great place to enjoy a cup of specialty coffee, or try one of their homemade brunch and breakfast options. Think fresh smoothies, cinnamon toasted brioche with honey mascarpone and za'atar fried chicken.

27 Argyle St, Ullapool IV26 2UB | @cult.cafe.ullapool

ULLAPOOL SEAFOOD SHACK

With a daily changing menu informed by whatever is dropped off that morning by the fishermen, you can expect to find the freshest fish imaginable at Ullapool's much-loved Seafood Shack. Go hungry and feast on hand-dived scallops, Ullapool-smoked trout and homemade cullen skink soup (a Highlands must, see page 26).

9 W Argyle St, Ullapool IV26 2TY

SUTOR CREEK CAFE

This Cromarty stalwart is known for its satisfying breakfasts, hearty lunches, homemade cakes and wood-fired pizzas. We particularly love their sweet things, which include lemon meringue pies, chocolate tarts, tiramisu, and rhubarb and pistachio cheesecakes. The chefs go foraging in the local area for the freshest ingredients to use in their seasonal menus.

21 Bank St, Cromarty IV11 8YE | @sutor_creek

Ullapool Seafood Shack

SLAUGHTERHOUSE COFFEE

The coffee served at this independent café is roasted right next door by Vandyke Bros. It's a great place to grab a perfectly-made flat white, brewed using local waters, and sip it on the shore of the Cromarty Firth.

Marine Terrace North (next to the ferry slipway), Cromarty IV11 8XZ | @slaughterhousecoffee

BAKHOOS BAKERY

Located in charming Fortrose and run by husband and wife team Scott Mackenzie and Charlotte King, Bakhoos is a beloved local bakery specialising in sourdough bread, viennoiserie, cakes and specialty coffee. Their focus is on quality and seasonal ingredients, so they change their menu regularly to showcase the best flavours of each season. Pick up crusty sourdough loaves, cardamom buns, flaky croissants, creative pastries (the feta, honey, sesame and nigella seed was a favourite), or one of their sandwiches made with their perfect focaccia.

85 High St, Fortrose IV10 8TX | bakhoosbakery.com @bakhoosbakery

Slaughterhouse Coffee

SLEEP

THE DIPPING LUGGER

You might find it hard to leave Ullapool, the picture-perfect fishing town on the shores of Lochbroom. It's small but bustling, with plenty of great places to eat fresh seafood, drink local whisky and befriend the lovely locals. For a luxurious yet laid back stay, The Dipping Lugger is unmissable. This 'Highland Home' faces the water and the mountains beyond, and has three cosy, elegant rooms upstairs equipped with plush super king beds and opulent bathrooms with free standing baths. Downstairs, their acclaimed restaurant serves a curated drinks list (including Seven Crofts gin, which owners Helen Chalmers and Robert Hicks make), and a menu that showcases the finest ingredients from the surrounding land. Ours included succulent lamb, perfect scallops, buttery turbot and a playful Lanark Blue cheese dish we can't stop talking about. And in the morning guests are treated to breakfasts of homemade granola, house-cured salmon and fresh apple juice from a nearby orchard. Even if you don't stay, be sure to book a meal here. It will be one of the culinary highlights of your trip.

4 W Shore St, Ullapool IV26 2UR | thedippinglugger.co.uk | @thedippinglugger

WATERFELL

This eco-friendly, bespoke retreat was built in 2021. Clean, modern architectural finishes make it a serene space to watch the waters of Loch Broom from your windows. It's right on the North Coast 500, and is an idyllic place to spend a few nights along the way. Sleeps up to two (in a super king bed, of course), with a three-night minimum.

Waterfell at Sealoch House, Loggie, Lochbroom, By Ullapool IV23 2SG
waterfell.co.uk

NEWHALL MAINS

Once operating as a farm building, Newhall Mains has been renovated but still retains its gothic heritage. You'll be able to take in views of the Black Isle peninsula's rolling hills and barley fields. Newhall Mains is made up of five cottages and four hotel suites in an eighteenth-century building and coach house. There is also a beautiful restaurant, whisky bar and private airfield on site. Just in case.

Newhall Mains Balblair, By Dingwall IV7 8LQ | newhall-mains.com
@newhallmains

The Dipping Lugger

EXPLORE

WANDER: GAIRLOCH

Spend a couple of hours exploring this charming village, which sits on the shore of Loch Gairloch. Many people use it as a base to explore Wester Ross, an area of outstanding natural beauty brimming with hidden hill lochs, misty mountain peaks and sweeping beaches – particularly the wide, white-sanded expanse of Big Sand. The village itself has lots of classic architecture and a few places to eat, drink and be merry. We recommend The Old Inn for the latter.

IV21 2BS

SHOP: HILLBILLIES BOOKSTORE

If you are passing through Gairloch (see above), grab a coffee from The Mountain Coffee Company before perusing this tiny bookshop, stocked with fiction, non-fiction, travel and mountaineering books, all hand-picked by the friendly staff.

Gairloch IV21 2BZ

SEE: GRUINARD BAY

A dramatic sweep of coast found along the North Coast 500 route, Gruinard Bay boasts rocky coves and three pink sand beaches from the Torridon rocks. A patchwork of little islands lie across the waters, which are lined by the Coigach Hills, with views out towards the fabled An Teallach mountain and the northern Highlands.

Nearest postcode: IV22 2NG

TOUR: BLACK ISLE BREWERY

Black Isle Brewery is a renowned craft brewery, beloved for their delicious and eco-friendly beers. They proudly source local ingredients, including organic barley and hops, to create their distinctive range. Drop by the brewery to sample (and probably fill your boot with) a range of beers, from classics to seasonal and experimental brews.

Old Allangrange, Munlochy IV8 8NZ | blackislebrewery.com

Black Isle Brewery

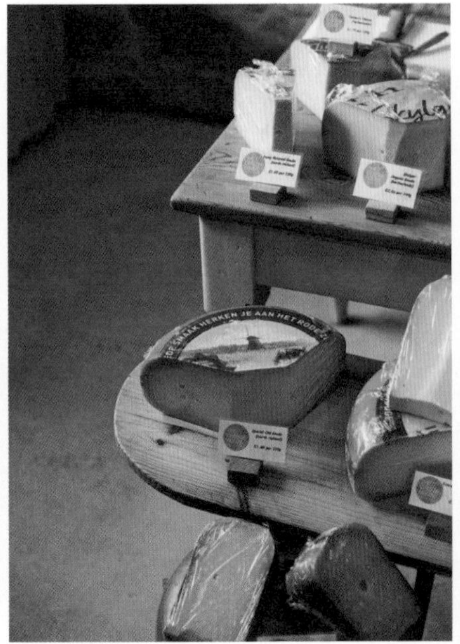

The Cheese House

BIKE: ULLAPOOL BIKE HIRE

Yes, there are hills in every direction. But if you fancy working up a sweat and being rewarded with jaw-dropping views of Loch Broom and The Fannichs, hire a mountain bike and set out a good few hours to explore. Or opt for one of their e-bikes if you want the same adventure, minus the sore legs.

Shore St, Ullapool IV26 2SZ | ullapoolbikehire.co.uk | @ullapoolbikehire

SEE: CHANONRY POINT

Spotting a dolphin is high on many people's agendas when visiting the Highlands' coastal regions, but it can be hard to know where to start. An Ullapool local told us Chanonry Point was our best bet. It's a narrow peninsula between Fortrose and Rosemarkie on the Black Isle, with beautiful views across the Moray Firth to Fort George. You'll find lots of dolphin spotters here, and the best time to try your luck is on a rising tide. If you do see them, they'll be just metres away from you. The best viewing point is just behind the lighthouse on the little shingle beach.

Nearest postcode: IV10 8SD

TOUR: CROMARTY BREWING CO.

Based in the beautiful Cromarty Firth, this family-run brewery has picked up more than a few awards for their innovative small batch beers, all handcrafted here. They stay away from chemicals and use the finest natural ingredients, which is why everything from their core range to their limited edition beers are brimming with flavour.

Davidston, Cromarty IV11 8XD | cromartybrewing.com

SHOP: THE CHEESE HOUSE

Let the passionate folks at The Cheese House (located in an old police station) teach you a thing or two about Gouda and goat's cheese at this award-winning shop in Cromarty. The town has a long trading history, and this place is the only UK importer of a unique range of artisan Dutch cheeses.

Old Police Station, Bank Street, Cromarty IV11 8UY | cromartycheese.com

SUTHERLAND
AND
CAITHNESS

SUTHERLAND AND CAITHNESS

This region includes some of the northernmost parts of the UK, including Dunnet Head and John O'Groats. It is also home to some of the wildest places in the Highlands, such as Suilven and Stac Pollaidh, with their staggering 3000 million-year-old rocks and hills. Architectural Pictish and Norse remains are scattered across the rugged landscape, which is primed for climbing, trekking, biking and star-gazing.

EAT AND DRINK

SOVI'S COFFEE HUT

Whether you're starting your ascent to Bones Caves or just need a coffee hit, Sovi's has you covered. This little wooden coffee cart beside a trickling burn (little river) serves great homemade cakes, Tea Pigs brews and excellent coffee.

Allt nan Uamh car park, Lairg IV27 4HL | @sovis_coffee

SHOREHOUSE RESTAURANT

Just five minutes off the North Coast 500 route, the family run Shorehouse Restaurant is must for seafood lovers. Our favourite is the seafood platter, a feast of fresh Handa prawns, local crab, smoked salmon and smoked mackerel, served with hot buttered potatoes.

Shorehouse Seafood Restaurant, Tigh Na Mara, Tarbet, Lairg IV27 4SS
shorehousetarbet.co.uk

Sovi's Coffee Hut

SLEEP

KYLESKU HOTEL

Kylesku is a boutique hotel on the shores of Loch Glendhu, overlooking the mountains surrounding this remote fishing hamlet. This former coaching inn is now a popular choice for those travelling the famous North Coast 500 route. If you aren't staying at the hotel, you can still visit the restaurant – which serves dishes inspired by traditional Scottish cuisine, highlighting locally sourced ingredients such as fresh seafood and locally reared meats.

Sutherland, Lairg IV27 4HW | kyleskuhotel.co.uk | @kylesku_hotel

LUNDIES HOUSE

This unimaginably idyllic hotel was once a manse – a home built for a local Christian minister. It still retains a sort of church-like serenity, overlooking hills laced with stone walls, the crumbling ruins of Castle Varrich and the wide loch beyond. Every inch of the place has been thoughtfully re-imagined in what can only be described as 'Scandi-Scot'. Buttery almond and golden apple coloured walls, flagstone floors, sash windows with candles flickering in the spring evening light. A spiral staircase leads to the bedrooms upstairs. Ours had the same flagstone floors, a giant bed topped with washed linen, a roll top bath set against a hand-painted wall mural and a window seat overlooking the water.

Guests sip classic cocktails with a Highland twist in the living room in the evenings, with music drifting through the rooms. The walls of the dining room are hand painted by French artist Claire Basler, depicting dreamy clouds and tangles of blossom. Dinner is different every night, showcasing local produce and shifting with the seasons – we ate sweet local langoustines, handmade tortellini in a rich, clear consommé, and Highland lamb three ways (including a crumbly bonbon we can't stop talking about). The candles flickered the next morning too, when breakfast included the orangest of local eggs on nutty toast, with buttery smoked salmon, homemade granola and soft, glistening chocolate and black sesame Danish morning buns. There's a feeling that you could while away hours on the sofa here, get lost in the lush, flower-filled grounds and fall asleep in front of the fire, local whisky in hand. The staff, with manager Nathan at its helm, make every moment indulgent yet effortlessly relaxed. Which is why we found it almost impossible to leave, and spent the next leg of the car journey plotting our return.

Lundies House, Tongue, Lairg IV27 4XF | Lundies.scot | @lundies.scot

Lundies House

EXPLORE

WALK: KNOCKAN CRAG NATURE RESERVE

One of the most unforgettable parts of the Highlands, if you ask us. You can touch 500 million years of geological history here. The dramatic landscape was formed by the Moine Thrust, the force of two continents crashing together. The Knockan Crag Trail is a one-hour walk that takes you up past the exposed rocks towards the top of the Knockan Crag, past sculptures and rocks carved with the poetry of Norman MacCaig. Up at the top, there are spectacular views over Loch Assynt.

Car park: Knockan Crag, Elphin, Lairg IV27 4HH

SEE: BONE CAVES AT INCHNADAMPH

Experience prehistoric Highlands in this surreal set of natural caves, set into a high limestone cliff in Inchnadamph, on the shores of Loch Assynt. The walk up to the cliff takes around an hour, with stunning views of the surrounding landscape. Inside, you'll be able to see the diverse animal life that once existed in this part of the world, including millennia-old fossils of Eurasian Lynx, polar bears, arctic fox and reindeer.

Car park: Allt nan Uamh Car Park, Lairg IV27 4HL

SEE: ARDVECK CASTLE

Park up next to A837 to wander down the footpath to this ruinous (but no less magnificent) castle. Ardvreck Castle dates back to around 1490, built on a rocky promontory jutting into the huge Loch Assynt. A lovely place to stop, listen to the lapping water and experience a piece of fifteenth-century Highlands history.

Lairg IV27 4HL

Knockan Crag Nature Reserve

BOAT: NORTHWEST SEA TOURS

Setting off from Kylesku Harbour, these wildlife and wilderness tours are run by a skipper with 35 years on the sea under his belt. You'll see Eas a'Chual Aluinn, Britain's highest waterfall – which is over three times higher than Niagara Falls – as well as lochs Glencoul and Glendhu. And if you're lucky you'll spot wildlife such as sea birds, sea eagles, puffins and seals. Tours take an hour and a half.

Kylesku Harbour, Sutherland IV27 4HW | northwestseatours.co.uk

SEE: BALNAKEIL CRAFT VILLAGE

This is the most northwesterly community on mainland Britain. Formerly a disused military camp, it was converted in the 1970s into a creative community of artists and makers. You'll find it along the North Coast 500 route, and it's a lovely place to stop. The village includes small art galleries, printmaking studios, ceramics, glasswork and woodwork, set against the glorious cliffs around the peninsula of Faraid Head.

Craft Village, Balnakeil, Durness, Lairg IV27 4PT
balnakeilcraftvillage.weebly.com

SEE: OLDSHOREMORE BEACH

This spectacular curved bay is known locally as Am Mellan. Its blindingly white sand is thanks to eroded stones and crushed seashells, and the clear blue waters are broken by rocky outcrops. The perfect beach to spread out on the sand and read a book for an entire afternoon.

Oldshoremoore, Lairg IV27 4R

SEE: CEANNABEINNE BEACH

Another jewel of a beach. It has white sands surrounded by rocky outcrops on its secluded shore, and the water is crystal clear on a sunny day. It lies beneath Beinn Ceannabeinne, a mountain with an elevation of 383 metres, and is hugged by cliffs of pink rock. Set up a picnic spot on the sloped cliff face in the evening for perfect sunset views over the sea. It's also a popular spot for wild campers, so you can expect to see a few people setting up their spot for the night.

Nearest postcode: IV27 4QE

Ceannabeinne Beach

SEE: BALNAKEIL BEACH

You'll find this wide, pristine beach near Cape Wrath just north of Durness. Banked by huge dunes, it's the perfect spot to let your dog run wild on the sand. Park at the beautiful ruins of Balnakeil Church and take the two-hour circular walk around Balnakeil Beach and the Faraid Head peninsula.

Durness, Lairg IV27 4PX

SEE: FORSINARD FLOWS

This nature reserve unfolds across a vast area surrounding Forsinard, right in the heart of the Flow Country – a large, rolling area of peatland. It might not sound too exciting, but this amber-coloured blanket bog is staggeringly vast and beautiful, with thousands of pools spread out across the land as far as the eye can see. Take the Forsinard Flows and Tower trail, a short 45-minute walk that crosses the blanket bog on a wooden walkway to visit the tower overlooking the mystifying landscape. After that, you can continue along a flagstone trail towards the bird- and plant-rich Dubh Lochan pools.

Forsinard Flows, Flows Field Centre, Forsinard KW13 6YT

SEE: FARR BEACH

Something of a hidden gem, this white sand beach can be found along the North Coast 500 route. Near Bettyhill on the north coast, it's a perfect place to try kayaking, body boarding or just a good old fashioned swim, and it's home to plenty of wildlife such as otters, golden eagles and seabird colonies.

A836, Bettyhill, Thurso KW14 7SS

SEE: STRATHY BEACH

Around spring and summer, wild flowers bloom on the hilltops lining this remote beach high on the northern coast. This wild expanse of sand stretches ½ mile (0.8 km) out into the Atlantic Ocean, banked by a wall of grassy dunes. It's a popular place for surfers in the winter, as it's protected from big swells and strong winds. The car park is just a five-minute walk away.

Car park: Thurso KW14 7RZ

SURF: SURFING IN THURSO

Thurso is renowned among surfing enthusiasts worldwide, with spots such as Thurso East providing challenging and powerful conditions. Despite the (very) cold waters, surfing in Thurso offers raw and untamed conditions for keen surfers, surrounded by stunning cliffs and breathtaking scenery. If you're looking to learn or improve your skills, North Coast Watersports (*www.northcoastwatersports.com*) offers great surf lessons, with expert guidance and equipment.

Thurso KW14 8BL

SHOP: COCOA MOUNTAIN

Discover a deliciously wide range of hand crafted chocolate bars, truffles and other delights. Founded in 2006, Cocoa Mountain handcrafts each chocolate using zero artificial flavourings, colourings or preservatives. Need to warm up? Their hot chocolate is the very thing.

8 Balnakeil, Durness, Craft IV27 4PT | cocoamountain.co.uk
@cocoamountain

SEE: TARBAT NESS

This candy cane-esque lighthouse was built by famous Scottish civil engineer Robert Stevenson in 1830. You'll find it standing strong on the northwest tip of the Tarbat Ness peninsula, close to the sleepy fishing village of Portmahomack. You can walk from the village to the lighthouse in about two and a half hours, with beautiful views of Dornoch Forth towards the Caithness coast along the way. Or just park up near the lighthouse to pay it a quick visit if you don't have time to walk.

Tain IV20 1RD

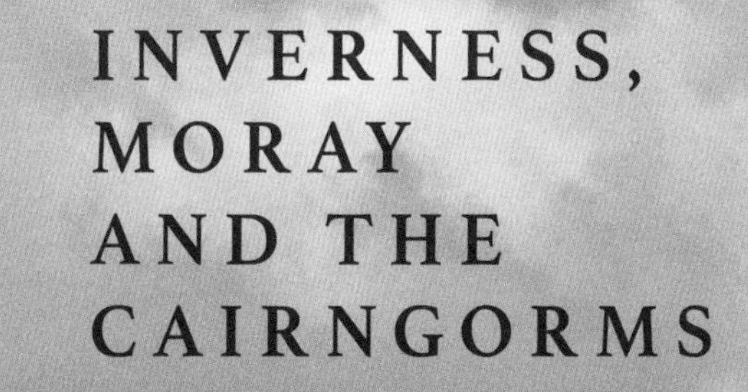

INVERNESS, MORAY AND THE CAIRNGORMS

INVERNESS, MORAY AND THE CAIRNGORMS

As you move into these regions, you'll notice the rocky, towering mountains turn into greener hills, with lush wedges of land jutting out towards the northeastern coast. The roads are shaded by soaring pine trees, and endless stretches of forest provide the perfect setting for sleepy cabin hideaways. Moray Speyside, with Aberdeenshire to the east and The Cairngorms to the south, is known as 'Whisky Country'. Most famous for being the home of malt whisky, more than half of Scotland's whisky distilleries can be found here. The Cairngorms National Park is unmissable, and boasting more lofty mountain ground than anywhere else in the UK. Dedicate at least a day to exploring this phenomenal place – and if you like a hike, this may well be your favourite destination. Over in the UK's northernmost city, Inverness, you can feast on local delicacies, pick up unique gifts, walk the bridges over River Ness and peruse some stunning classical architecture.

EAT AND DRINK

MACGREGOR'S BAR

If you ask an Inverness local where to drink, they'll most likely point you in the direction of this much-loved bar. Hand-selected Scottish craft beers and whiskies are served in a glowy bar with stone walls and a wood burner. They have a food menu of local, seasonal dishes too. Combine this with daily live music events and the odd famous musician tucked in the corner, and you've got one of Scotland's most memorable bars. We guarantee you'll end up staying longer than you planned to.

109–113 Academy St, Inverness IV1 1LX | macgregorsbars.com
@macgregorsbar

VELOCITY CAFÉ

This social enterprise is made up of a friendly bicycle workshop and vegetarian café. Using local and seasonal produce, they serve breakfast, brunch and lunch, along with coffee from Glasgow's Papercup Roasters. They have a zero-waste mission and host regular projects encouraging sustainable living, cycling and waste reduction.

1 Crown Avenue, Inverness IV2 3NF | velocitylove.co.uk
@velocityinverness

CROWN & ANCHOR INN

A classic, cosy boozer overlooking Findhorn bay. Crown & Anchor specialise in classic Scottish cooking, making use of fresh Moray seafood, locally sourced meat and seasonal vegetables, along with roughly 120 malt whiskies served in their Whisky Bar.

44 Findhorn, Moray IV36 3YE | crownandanchorinn.co.uk

BATCHEN STREET COFFEE

Fuel up on award-winning specialty coffee, served from this coffee shop and roastery in Elgin. They hand-roast their coffee in small batches, which they also sell in bags to take home. As well as seriously good coffee, they also make delicious things such as breakfast naans, eggs benedict made with organic eggs, fluffy French toast and luxurious single origin hot chocolate.

33 Batchen St, Elgin IV30 1BH | batchenstreetcoffee.uk
@batchenstreetcoffee

Above and below: *Cairngorms and The Boath House*

SLEEP

KILLIEHUNTLY FARMHOUSE & COTTAGES

A laid-back (but luxurious) hideout of guesthouse and self-catered cottages in the wilds of the Cairngorm National Park. Whitewashed walls, vases of greenery, flickering candles and a wild sauna yurt give this place a Scandi feel, while a larder full of local produce and outdoor experiences allow you to immerse yourself in the beauty of the area.

Killiehuntly Farmhouse, Killiehuntly, Kingussie PH21 1NZ | @killiehuntly.scot killiehuntly.scot

BOATH HOUSE RESTAURANT AND ROOMS

Manicured lawns lead to the door of this Grade A-listed Palladian hotel. But inside, everything is refreshingly paired back, minimal and flooded with natural light. There are 10 bedrooms in the main house, all designed to inspire calm and creativity for the artists that often stay here. There's also a four-bedroom self-catered lodge, restaurant, sixteenth-century writing studio and a painting studio on the banks of the Boath burn. Owner Jonny Gent opened Clerkenwell's celebrated Sessions Arts Club along with Florence Knight in 2021. A year later, Boath House opened. Food-lovers flock to its 400-year-old walled garden café. It's a daydream of clean white walls, a corrugated iron bar and an open kitchen serving re-imagined Scottish classics using local produce and ingredients grown on the grounds. We had a springtime feast of raspberry negronis, flatbread topped with wild garlic pesto, cullen skink with velvety leek oil and mussels in cider sauce made using apples from their orchard.

Auldearn, Nairn IV12 5TE | boath-house.com | @boathhouse

CALLIE BOTHY

Imagine camping in a dense, pine-scented forest crawling with Highland gorse. But instead of a tent, you're sleeping in a contemporary bothy with a plush bed, squishy sofa, fully-equipped kitchen and giant bathtub. Callie Bothy is a woodland retreat where you can bathe in the natural surroundings, with all the luxuries of a hotel suite. Hidden down a winding woodland path deep in Moray Speyside, this isolated bothy has a postbox-red front door, piles of chopped wood, a wraparound deck and smoke curling from the chimney. Callie was built by hand by owners Alie and Phil, using sustainable materials that match the surrounding land. Outside, there's a wood-fired hot tub and firepit overlooking the pond, perfect for evening beers. Inside, floor to ceiling windows offer full views of the woodland, and you can watch the trees shivering in the night sky as you bathe.

Lower Calliemuckie, Pluscarden, Elgin, Moray IV30 8TZ | calliebothy.scot

Callie Bothy

EXPLORE

SHOP: LEAKEY'S BOOKSHOP

While away a couple of hours exploring the shelves of Scotland's biggest secondhand bookshop. Leakey's is a stone's throw from the River Ness, and has been a family-owned business since 1979. They sell just about everything here, including collectables, all the classics, poetry, maps and prints, plus signed editions of rare books. It's a joyful space, with sky blue ceilings, spiral staircases and a roaring fireplace in the centre. There's even a reading space upstairs, complete with cosy sofas. Can we move in?

Church St, Inverness IV1 1EY | leakeysbookshop.com
@leakeysbookshop

SEE: NAIRN BEACH

Nairn is a charming seaside resort 16 miles (26 km) east of Inverness. It gets busy in the summer, when visitors flock to this giant sandy beach that stretches eastwards towards Moray. It's fringed by sand dunes and a grassy hinterland, with rock pools dotted across the sands. If you get hungry, head to Nairn's nearby promenade directly behind the beach, where you'll find some lovely cafés.

Nairn IV12 4EA

TOUR: GLENFIDDICH DISTILLERY

Speyside is home to the world's largest concentration of Scotch malt whisky distilleries, and lots of people come here to follow the 'Malt Whisky Trail'. If you just want to visit one or two, Glenfiddich is a good place to start. You'll probably already be aware of Glenfiddich; it's the most awarded single malt Scotch whisky in the world, and one of Scotland's last family-owned distilleries. Drop in for a guided tour of the spectacular grounds – complete with tastings, of course.

Dufftown, Keith AB55 4DH | glenfiddich.com/distillery
@glenfiddichdistillery

SEE: FINDHORN BEACH

Don't miss this long, uninterrupted stretch of sparkling white sand. This idyllic beach is near the village of Findhorn, with views of the mountains on the other side of the Moray Firth. Bring a pair of binoculars and you might just spy some seals across the bay.

Nearest postcode: IV36 3YE | Or park at The Captain's Table and walk from there: Findhorn Marina, Moray, Forres IV36 3YE

The Glenfiddich Distillery

SEE: DUFFAS CASTLE

Standing proudly on a hill, Duffas Castle was in use from 1140 to 1705, and is the best-preserved example of a medieval moat-and-bailey style structure. You'll find it about 3 miles (4.8 km) northwest of Elgin.

Elgin IV30 5RH

SHOP: WINDSWEPT BREWING CO.

With their passion for quality and respect for traditions, this small independent brewery crafts hop-forward ales and robust stouts that smack of the Highlands. They have a welcoming taproom where you can sample their creations and pick up a few bottles of their award-winning beers to take home.

Unit B 13 Coulardbank Industrial Estate, Lossiemouth IV31 6NG
windsweptbrewing.com | @windsweptbrewing

SHOP: PENCIL ME IN

A place as beautiful as the Highlands deserves to be written about. If you're struck by the desire to put pen to paper, head to 'Scotland's favourite stationary shop' in Elgin. They stock brands such as Kaweco and Standard Issue, along with project notebooks from The School of Life, colourful prints and not-boring birthday cards. Pick up a shiny new pen and notebook, then park yourself at Batchen Street coffee next door for a writing session.

27 Batchen St, Elgin IV30 1BH | pencilmeinshop.co.uk | @pencilmeinshop

SEE: SPEYSIDE COOPERAGE

As soon as you arrive at Speyside Cooperage, you'll be greeted by the sights and sounds of coopers hammering, shaping and charring barrels. Take a guided tour to learn about the process of barrel making, from selecting the finest oak to witnessing the centuries-old intricate craftsmanship that goes into creating these essential vessels for maturing whisky. It's a little like stepping back in time.

Dufftown Road, Craigellachie, Banffshire, Keith AB38 9RS
speysidecooperage.co.uk

TOUR: THE BALVENIE DISTILLERY

Tours are by appointment only here, and last two and a half hours. Learn about Balvenie's use of centuries-old whisky making. Balvenie (meaning 'village of luck') was founded in 1892, and they are the only distillery in the Highlands that still abides by the Five Rare Crafts of whisky making – namely home-grown barley, crafted casks, a traditional malting floor, copper stills and a malt master.

Balvenie Maltings, Dufftown, Keith AB55 4BB | thebalvenie.com | @thebalvenie

WALK: MEAL A'BHUACHAILLE VIA RYVOAN BOTHY

For stunning views of the Cairngorms National Park, begin this half day walk at the Forestry Commission Visitor Centre in Glenmore. Walk steeply up towards the bealach (mountain pass) between Creagan Gorm and Meal a'Bhuachaille, where you'll be able to drink in the views across Loch Morlich to the Cairngorm massif. Following the unmarked trail beyond, you'll come down to Ryvoan Bothy, a former croft abandoned in 1877, and taken over by the Mountain Bothies Association in 1972. This one-roomed mountain bothy is a great example of a classic walker's resting place, probably mostly used these days as a brief stop for casual walkers. Beyond the bothy, you'll pass the shores of An Lochan Uaine (Green Loch), before taking the high or low route back to the visitor centre through a pine forest rich with ancient trees.

Glenmore Visitor Centre car park: PH22 1QU | Buses run regularly between Aviemore and the Glenmore Visitor Centre (and continue to Cairngorm Mountain Railway), details at travelinescotland.com

TOUR: CAIRNGORM BREWERY

This craft brewery was launched back in 2001, and you can visit its original site in the village of Aviemore, tucked in the Cairngorms National Park. They work their magic on a great selection of Scottish craft beers, from a light beer to classic milk stout. Drop by for a taster session and pick up a few bottles to take home.

Dalfaber Industrial Estate, Aviemore PH22 1ST | cairngormbrewery.com

ABERDEENSHIRE, ANGUS AND EAST CAIRNGORMS

ABERDEENSHIRE, ANGUS AND EAST CAIRNGORMS

With its broad Highland glens and gorgeous seashore, Angus, north of Dundee, is the gateway to Aberdeenshire. In winter, skiers hit the slopes at Glenshee and Lecht, and you'll find picturesque villages to explore and forest trails to wander year-round, as well as plenty of great food and drink. The East Cairngorms, home to Braemar and Ballater in Royal Deeside, have picturesque mountains, clear rivers and native forests, making it a dramatic – and addictive – place to visit.

EAT AND DRINK

TARMACHAN CAFE

If you're passing through the riverside village of Crathie in the Cairngorms National Park, be sure to stop by for lunch at Tarmachan Cafe. It was designed by the architectural studio next door, made up of clean lines, black wood and serene minimalist interiors, nestled among the silver birch and juniper. Artisan coffee is served alongside freshly baked sourdough sandwiches, pastries and very addictive Balmoral venison sausage rolls. Closed on Sundays and Mondays.

Quarry Studios, Crathie AB35 5UL | tarmachancafe.com | @tarmachan_cafe

FISH SHOP

Located in Ballater, this royal blue restaurant and adjoining fishmonger celebrates the timeworn traditions of Scottish fishing. The menu changes daily, always offering classic but creative seafood dishes using fish sourced ethically from short boat trips, along with creel-caught and hand-dived crustacea.

3 Netherley Place, Ballater AB35 5QE | fishshopballater.co.uk
@fishshopballater

ROTHESAY ROOMS

Led by acclaimed chef Scott Smith, this restaurant aims to capture Scotland's culinary heritage using locally sourced ingredients and sustainable practices. Think succulent West Coast scallops and Highland venison, served in a forest green dining room adorned with dark wood and touches of tartan. Be sure to book.

Station Square, Ballater AB35 5RB | rothesay-rooms.co.uk
@rothesayrooms

THE BAY

Craving classic fish and chips? The Bay is your next stop. Found on the coast in Stonehaven, which is worth a visit in itself, this ever popular spot serves up top quality, properly traditional fish and chips. They use the freshest fish sourced locally, and their portions are satisfyingly huge.

Beach Promenade, Stonehaven AB39 2RD | thebayfishandchips.co.uk
@thebayfish

Tarmachan Cafe

AUNTY BETTY'S

Having gained a cult following for their small-batch, handmade ice creams, you'll most likely find a queue outside Aunty Betty's – even in the rain. Choose from classics such as vanilla and chocolate to Scottish tablet, lavender honey and blood orange sorbet. Their sundaes, hot chocolates and milkshakes are pretty amazing.

Aunty Bettys, The Promenade, Stonehaven AB39 2RD
auntybettys.co.uk | @auntybettystonehaven

THE LOBSTER SHOP

Grabbing a lobster roll from The Lobster Shop and eating it on the beach with a cold beer is an unmissable pleasure. This fish shop (and a takeaway in the summer months) specialises in responsibly-caught lobster and crab, which you can eat there or take home with you. Arrive early in the summer to avoid missing out on Ruth's famous lobster salad and katsu crab rolls. Closed on Mondays and Tuesdays.

Fore St, Johnshaven, Montrose DD10 0EU | thelobster.shop
@johnshavenlobstershop

THE SEAFOOD BOTHY

Operating out of a former rice horsebox on Stonehaven's historic harbour, this is the place to grab a filling lunch of the freshest seafood. The menu changes according to what's been caught that morning, but expect big plates of lobster, langoustines and crab, with lots of delicious sides.

Stonehaven Harbour AB39 2JU | @seafoodbothy

HAZELNUT PÂTISSERIE

Right next door to Braemar Brewing Co. (see page 139) is this light-flooded pâtisserie. It's run by classically-trained pastry chef Mathilde and master coffee maker Ros, two friends who met while working down the road at The Fife Arms (see page 134). Their pâtisseries combine Scottish flavours with classic French techniques. Think black forest gâteau, lemon tart and golden hazelnut choux. They also make perfectly crumbly quiche, amazing coffee and stuffed croissants.

Airlie House, Chapel Brae, Braemar, AB35 5YT
hazelnut-braemar.com | @hazelnutpatisserie

Hazelnut Pâtisserie

SLEEP

THE FIFE ARMS

We weren't expecting to be sipping oolong tea underneath Picasso's *Femme assise dans un fauteuil* when we dropped into The Fife Arms. Or to see a Lucien Freud portrait, a collection of Man Ray photographs, or a delicate watercolour by Queen Victoria. But it all makes sense when you learn that this former hunting lodge was renovated by Iwan and Manuela Wirth, the couple behind the world-renowned gallery Hauser & Wirth. There are 46 guestrooms and suites upstairs, while downstairs guests and visitors can revel in a little 'Highlands Hedonism' in the Art Deco Elsa Schiaparelli cocktail bar, eat wood-fired delicacies in The Clunie Dining Room (with a wall mural painted by Guillermo Kuitca), sip whisky in the sumptuous Bertie's Whisky Bar, or rub shoulders with Braemar locals at their very own pub, The Flying Stag. There are daily art tours, led by the warmest staff decked out in tartan and marigold ties. The whole place is magical, with surprises round every corner. And while it brims with luxury, it also feels like walking into a very familiar home… somehow.

Mar Rd, Braemar AB35 5YN | thefifearms.com | @thefifearms

GLEN DYE CABINS

'Keep Glen Dye a secret' is muralled in fuschia across the back of Glen Dye's main house. It sums up the feeling of the place; a home away from home tucked in the forest. Across the 30,000 acre estate, there is a collection of converted cabins and cottages sleeping from two to seven guests. There's several styles of cabin, including two that are part of a Victorian shooting lodge on the banks of the River Dye, stylish holiday homes crafted from derelict farm buildings, and The Saw Mill, where guests sleep in a refurbished 1950's American Airstream Safari trailer. Everyone has access to their own private hot tub, and can book a slot to use the sauna hidden among the trees. Our personal favourite feature is The Glen Dye Arms, the on-site BYOB pub complete with roaring log fire, ancient bar and record player. Perfect for winding down after a day exploring the surrounding wilderness. This colourful oasis is just 40 minutes from Aberdeen, but it feels like its own world.

Bridge of Dye Steading, Strachan, Banchory AB31 6LT
glendyecabinsandcottages.com | @glendyecabinsandcottages

The Fife Arms

EXPLORE

SKI: GLENSHEE AND LECHT SKI CENTRES

When the snow hits Aberdeenshire, its mountains and valleys come alive. You have plenty of options when it comes to tackling the slopes, but we recommend Glenshee and Lecht ski centres. Both are a 40-minute drive from Ballater. Glenshee covers over 2000 acres, spread across four spectacular mountains and three valleys. You'll have a choice of 36 runs, which includes the famously challenging black run, Tiger. The Lecht has something for every kind of skier. It lies 2,090 feet (637 metres) above sea level in the Eastern Cairngorms. You can hire all your equipment online or at their centre, but be sure to book in advance. Scotland's ski season technically runs from December to early April, but conditions are best from January onwards.

visitballater.com/skiing

TOUR: ROYAL LOCHNAGAR DISTILLERY

Visit this classic distillery on the south side of the River Dee. It sits at the foot of the Cairngorm mountains, a mile from Balmoral Castle, and is fed by the clear water of the Scarnock springs. They use age-old craftsmanship to create one of the region's finest whiskies, which you can learn all about on one of their in-depth distillery tours.

Balmoral, Crathie, Ballater, Aberdeenshire AB35 5TB
malts.com/en-row/distilleries/royal-lochnagar

SHOP: TOR WORKSHOP

This warm, minimal furniture showroom in Braemar is also a whisky tasting room, so it's worth a visit even if you aren't planning to invest in some of their bespoke pieces. Tor was founded by brothers Tom and Ben Addy, whose actual workshop lies on the banks of the River Muick. They follow the ethos of 'Sharp Tools, Keen Eye'. They make use of diseased and dead standing timber, and are inspired by the surrounding natural landscape. Drop by to take a look at some of their beautiful pieces, and sample some lovingly-selected whisky while you're there.

The Mews, Braemar AB35 5YL | torworkshop.com
@tor.workshop

Tor Workshop

Linn of Dee

SHOP: BRAEMAR CHOCOLATE

Often using local ingredients such as whisky, bread and even cheese, Braemar Chocolate showcases the diversity and quality of Scottish produce. Our favourite is the Highland bar, inspired by foraging for wild thyme; walnut ganache wrapped in milk chocolate, topped with caramelised thyme walnuts.

10 Invercauld Rd, Braemar AB35 5YP | braemarchocolateshop.co.uk
@braemarchocolate

TOUR: BRAEMAR BREWING CO.

Pale ale, golden ale, stout and seasonal ales are produced at this nano brewery in Braemar. Drop by for a chat with the head brewer, and pick up a few bottles for your next lochside picnic.

Airlie House Chapel, Brae, Braemar AB35 5YT GB | brewbraemar.uk
@brewbraemar

WALK: LINN OF DEE

This was one of our favourite walks of the whole trip. A beloved picnic spot of Queen Victoria, this area is part of the National Trust for Scotland. It has a handful of waymarked trails, which lead you through fairytale pinewoods carpeted with moss, past the gorge and along the River Dee. You might pass a few fellow walkers on your way, but for the most part it'll feel like you've been dropped into your own world.

Car park: Braemar AB35 5YJ

SEE: GREAT NORTH OF SCOTLAND RAILWAY BUILDING

We weren't surprised to see this eye-catching building featured in *Accidentally Wes Anderson*. The building's white and blue timber exterior and toy-town lettering looks like it's been plucked straight from one of his formalist films. Despite the signage, this was never actually a railway station. The Great North of Scotland Railway ran all the way to Scotland's northern coast in the mid nineteenth-century. It was intended to serve Braemar too, but the plans were altered in the 1860s. After that, the North of Scotland Railway started running bus services to remote towns like this in the early twentieth century. This bus depot is no longer in use, but its original features remain (just don't look at its rear). You can even take a peek into the original waiting room and office through the front windows.

Braemar AB35 5TS

SEE: THE WATCHERS INSTALLATION AND CORGARFF VIEWPOINT

Sixteenth-century Corgarff Castle's bone-white exterior stands in striking contrast to the rolling green hills of Aberdeenshire, where it sits in wild insolation. The best place to view this evocative scene is high up on Lecht Road, home to a viewpoint and two innovative art installations. 'A Moment in Time' is a tall standing stone, carved with poetry and designed to frame the view of the castle. More recently, The Watchers installation was added. These abstract steel cowels line the hillside, acting as hooded shelters from the wind and snow. They are peaceful places to sit and watch the eagles flying above the landscape.

Corgarff Castle Viewpoint: AB36 8YP

WALK: CAMBUS O'MAY FOREST TRAILS

You've got three circular trails to choose from in these pinewood forests, but we recommend taking the longest one, the Cambus o'May Pinewood Trail. Start in the forestry car park, where you'll find a good map showing you the route. You'll wind through an enchanting woods filled with towering Scots Pines and Grand Firs, past tree-fringed lochans, little stone bridges and plenty of picnic spots. You might spy some Red Squirrels or Capercaillie, and you'll be able to see up Deeside to the mountains beyond along the way. Most trails take around an hour and a half.

Car park: AB35 5SD

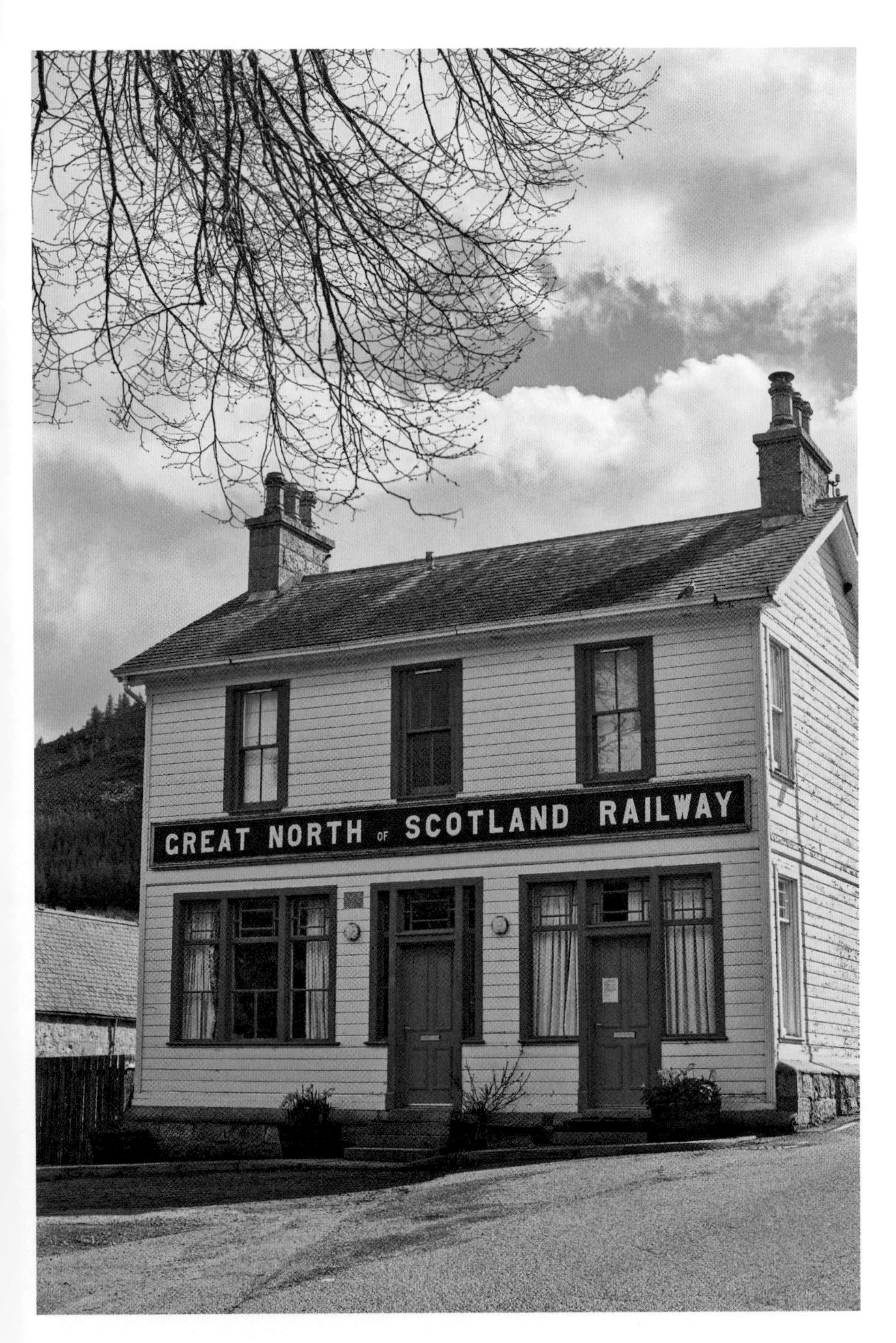

Great North of Scotland Railway Building

PERTHSHIRE

PERTHSHIRE

Highland Perthshire's lush green hills are home to thriving farm stays, perched high with endless views across the lands. There is less of the wild, craggy beauty of the west coast, but the region is brimming with historic charm.

GERANIUMS
£5
MIXED
BUNCHES
£15
LES MARAÎCHERS, de Nature ENGAGÉS, de Culture PASSIONNÉS

EAT AND DRINK

ANCASTER COFFEE

Get your hit of Scottish roast coffee, cakes and bakes in this Ancaster Square café in bustling Callander. There are plenty of comfy sofas inside if you feel like putting your feet up.

Ancaster Square, Callander FK17 8ED

GLEN LYON COFFEE

For the ultimate specialty coffee experience, make a pitstop at Glen Lyon in Aberfeldy. They roast all their coffee in small batches on site – in full view of everyone who walks through the door. They source their coffee ethically, working closely with farmers and co-operatives in over 12 countries, and every last bean is 100 per cent traceable. Founder Fiona is one of only a handful of Q graders in the UK, so she and her super senses make all the final decisions.

Aberfeldy PH15 2AQ | glenlyoncoffee.co.uk | @glenlyoncoffee

THE SCOTTISH DELI

Stock up on local goodies at this specialty food larder and gourmet sandwich shop. They have freshly ground Glen Lyon coffee, a great selection of wines, Scottish Gins and local craft beers. From 5.45pm, 'The Scottish Deli in the Evening' opens, serving up Scottish Deli tapas and treats.

1 Atholl St, Dunkeld PH8 0AR | scottish-deli.com

THE TAYBANK

Any locals would call this hotel, bar and restaurant the hub of Dunkeld. They have the biggest beer garden in Perthshire, featuring their Garden Kitchen, bar, coffee and ice cream hut all on the banks of the River Tay. Their colourful restaurant serves creative dishes informed by the Scottish seasons, with many of their ingredients grown in their walled garden in the grounds of Murthly Estate. Built in 1809, The Taybank has become known for its live music, with bustling live sessions in the downstairs bar every Wednesday evening and every other Sunday.

Tay Terrace, Dunkeld PH8 0AQ | thetaybank.co.uk | @thetaybank

The Taybank

ARAN BAKERY

Baker and owner Flora Shedden released *Aran: Recipes and Stories from a Bakery in the Heart of Scotland* in 2019. This much-loved book is based on the delicious goings-on at Flora's artisan bakery on Atholl Street, which she lives above. Everything on display in this soothing, whitewashed place is baked on site using local, seasonal produce supplied by friends and neighbours. Golden sausage rolls, flaky pastries, classics such as lemon meringue pie and beautiful creations like wild garlic and asparagus danishes. Our advice is simple: try as many things as you can.

2 Atholl St, Dunkeld PH8 0AR | aran-bakery.com | @aran_scott

REDWOOD WINES

Settle down for a few glasses at this cosy neighbourhood wine bar. Owners Roseanna and Morgwn Preston-Jones first met in New York in 2006. Morgwn hails from California, and worked at Moro in London before taking over the kitchens at Bedales Wines. Redwood showcases some of California's finest wines, alongside house-made charcuterie, artisanal cheeses and organic produce. Their food menu changes weekly, is informed by the seasons and made daily by hand. Chef Morgwn also leads monthly themed wine tastings, often with food pairings. The perfect way to spend an evening, we'd say.

12 Bridge St, Dunkeld PH8 0AH | redwoodwines.co.uk | @redwoodwines

Aran Bakery

SLEEP

LOCH VENACHAR CABINS

These luxury eco cabins are set right on the waterside. The handful of self-contained cabins are complete with full kitchens, en suite bathrooms, hot tubs, log fires and super king beds. Floor-to-ceiling glass and no blinds means you'll wake up with the sun, and sip your morning coffee overlooking the Trossachs National Park and Ben Venue.

Dullater Burnside, Invertrossachs FK17 8HP
lochvenacharcabins.co.uk | @loch_venachar_cabins

CORR CABINS @ MONACHYLE MHOR

Corr Cabins was born out of a desire for a better alternative to conventional glamping pods and outdated caravans. Frustrated by the lack of quality yet affordable cabin homes out there, the owners turned their focus toward creating minimal, stylish and fully-equipped cabins. This particular one can be found on the grounds of Monachlye Mhor. The black timber cabin features a king-size bed with panoramic mountain views, an ensuite with a large forest-view shower, a wood-burning stove, underfloor heating and an outdoor fire pit.

Balquhidder, Lochearnhead FK19 8PQ | corrcabins.com | @corr_cabins

MHOR84

Inspired by the roadside motels of North America, this motel restaurant, bar and café is the perfect stop on the A84 – otherwise known as the road to the Highlands. Walkers, cyclists and locals gather by the fire, in the sunny restaurant or out the front. Their menu changes every day and they source many ingredients from their very own farm at Monachyle Mhor. Expect big, fortifying breakfasts, seasonal lunches, oysters and classics such as steak or seafood chowder.

84 Kingshouse, Balquhidder, Lochearnhead FK19 8NY
mhor84.net | @mhor84

STRATHYRE
FESTIVAL
FRIDAY
SATURDAY
WWW.STRATHYREFESTIVAL.COM
Mr Whippy
Cone & Tub

Mhor84

BALLINTAGGART

Perfectly located in the lush, rolling hills of the Tay Valley in Perthshire, Ballintaggart is made up of two venues. There is the original Ballintaggart Farm, perched at the top of the valley, where guests can enjoy two cosy rooms, a huge kitchen, orchard and kitchen garden. This is also where you can hone your skills at Ballintaggart's famous Cook School. A five-minute drive down the road is the charming Grandtully Hotel with eight bedrooms, a cosy bar and a restaurant serving dishes brimming with 'big, seasonal flavours'.

Grandtully, Strathtay PH9 0PL | ballintaggart.com | @ballintaggart

GUARDSWELL FARM

Finishing our evening yoga class with a cup of fresh herbal tea, it's safe to say we'd reached peak relaxation after only a few hours at Guardswell Farm. This 150-acre grassland farm is perched on a hillside overlooking the Perthshire landscape. It's the perfect place to come and be very wholesome, since you'll be staying in one of their (very beautifully designed) off-grid cabins complete with stargazing windows, log burners and kingsize beds. They host events such as spoon carving and Open Farm Sundays, as well as evening yoga classes. There's a shop in the main building for any artisanal goods you might need to make your stay even more dreamy, from local cider to Hebridean biscuits, natural wine and incense.

Kinnaird, By Inchture PH14 9QZ | guardswell.co.uk | @guardswellfarm

Guardswell Farm

The Shop by Ballintaggart

EXPLORE

WANDER: KENMORE

This little village lines the northern shores of Loch Tay. The 14-mile (22.5 km) long loch is a popular destination for sailing, canoeing and water skiing. If you feel like going fishing, you'll find double bank fishing on 2½ miles (4 km) of the River Tay, starting at Kenmore Bridge. You can visit the stunning grounds of Taymouth Castle, and spot the towering peak of Ben Lawers on the horizon. There's a few hotels in the village, and if you're planning a picnic on the edge of the loch, head to Taymouth Courtyard Shop & Delicatessen to stock up on local produce and luxury hampers.

Taymouth Courtyard Shop & Delicatessen: Mains of Taymouth, 6 The Beeches, Kenmore, Aberfeldy PH15 2HN

SHOP: THE SHOP BY BALLINTAGGART

Stock up on signature Ballintaggart products such as their very own foraged gin, scented candles and preserves, as well as favourites from local Highland producers. They also sell beautiful gift hampers – preferably to give to yourself…

1 Dunkeld St, Aberfeldy PH15 2DA | shop.ballintaggart.com | @ballintaggart

TOUR: DEWARS DISTILLERY

Dewars' first single malt whisky was produced in 1898. Visit this historic distillery in the heart of Perthshire for a stroll around the scenic grounds, an interactive exhibition and, of course, a few nips of the good stuff.

Aberfeldy PH15 2EB | dewars.com

SHOP: ABERFELDY WATERMILL BOOKSHOP AND CAFE

First made famous by Robert Burns' 1787 song 'The Birks Of Aberfeldy', this little but lively town on Loch Tay is well worth a visit. While you're there, dip into this bookshop, café and gallery. It's located in a three-storey former oatmeal mill, with a huge selection of fiction and non-fiction books from Scottish and international writers. You can get great coffee and lunches of local produce in the café downstairs – the perfect place to flick through your new book. Next door, their homeware shop Homer stocks beautiful fabrics, cushions, candles and everything else you'll need to bring a slice of coorie back home with you.

Mill St, Aberfeldy PH15 2BG | aberfeldywatermill.com
@aberfeldywatermill

SHOP: THE WHISKY BOX

It would be all wrong to leave the Highlands without a bottle of whisky in your bag. If you're exploring Dunkeld, head to this independent whisky and craft beer shop, which also pairs as a tasting room, so you can sample a few Highland malts – or maybe a local gin, if that's more your thing.

2 High St, Dunkeld PH8 0AJ | dunkeldwhiskybox.co.uk

SHOP: LON STORE

Another dreamy venture from Aran's Flora Shedden (see page 148), this sunny store sells irresistible wares from Highland makers, fresh flowers and local ceramics, along with fresh produce, artisan chocolate, cheese, cider, coffee, preserves and just about everything else you could want to brighten your kitchen/soul.

4 High St, Dunkeld PH8 0AJ | lon-store.co.uk | @lonthestore

ARAN
FLORA SHEDD
LÓN
SUPPER
recipes worth staying in for
FLORA SHEDDEN
CAPERS
CAPERS
FEVER-TREE
CUCUMBER TONIC WATER
T
TONIC WATER
JEREMY LEE
COOKING
CHEFS' FRIDGES
SHIPTON MILL
SHIPTON MILL
DRINKS BISCUITS
J.J.MELLIS
Maldon
ACQUA PANNA
ACQUA PANNA
ALDER
WILD
guide

Lon Store

INDEX

GENERAL

CRAFTS

EAT & DRINK

EXPLORE

SHOPPING

SLEEP

MADE
BY THE SEA